⑥

"Maria gives hope to the human spirit. She has inspired many people, from all walks of life, to reach their highest potential. She has personally helped me to embrace the moments we are given. Her inspiring wisdom speaks to the heart. My life has changed for the better because of her help."

—LAURI HENDERSON, Los Angeles, California

⑥

"Maria helped me to make major career decisions a few years ago. My life is now turning out to be more exciting than I've ever imaged! She has also helped many of my friends, understand their life path and grow in positive ways. Everyone loves her! She touches a part of your soul, and gives you knowledge, to let go of negative patterns and self limitations. She has helped us to see that life can really be a wondrous adventure!"

—JULIE NEWVILLE, Ft Lauderdale, Florida
Regal USA, Artistic Director

⑥

"Maria is wonderful. I have been to many respected astrologers over the years but Maria has been the most accurate, especially with relationships. She knows her astrology but it's her intuitive insight that puts her ahead of the rest!"

—MEGAN WASLOWSKI, Denver Colorado

⑥

"When a friend first suggested I contact Maria for a reading, I was very skeptical. When she gave me the reading, I couldn't believe her accuracy. It was quite astonishing. I've since had regular consultations and now it just seems like I'm talking to a caring friend."

—ALLISON HAUMAN, England (UK)

About the Author

Maria Shaw is a professional astrologer and relationship counselor to thousands of people all over the world. This Cancer sun sign divides her time between residences in Michigan and New Orleans' historic French Quarter. A former television news anchor and reporter, she has also hosted her own syndicated television program. Currently, Maria travels around the country hosting seminars, lectures and workshops. She is married to a stubborn yet lovable, Taurus and has two creative water-sign daughters.

To Contact the Author

Visit Maria on her website www.MariaShaw.com

Or write to P.O. Box 490, Genesee MI 48437-0490

Every effort by Maria's staff will be made to answer all inquiries. Consultations and information on lectures and group seminars available.

To Order Additional
Copies of This Book:

Send $20 plus $3.20 for S&H per book to:
P.O. Box 490, Genesee, MI 48437-0490

HEART and SOUL

MARIA SHAW'S
Karmic Love and Compatibility Guide

Maria Shaw

Mid-Summers Eve Publishing

Heart and Soul,
Maria Shaw's Karmic Love and Compatibility Guide

Copyright © 2000 by Maria Shaw.

FIRST EDITION
First Printing, 2000

ISBN - 0-9704834-0-6

Publisher's Cataloging-in-Publication
(Provided by Quality Books, Inc.)

Shaw, Maria.
    Heart and soul : Maria Shaw's karmic love and
compatibility guide / Maria Shaw.—1st ed.
    p. cm.
    ISBN: 0-9704834-0-6

    1. Love—Miscellanea. 2. Mate selection—Miscellanea. 3. Karma.
4. Astrology and marriage. I. Title.

BF1729.L6S53 2000   133.5'81582
                                               QB100-828

Cover and interior design by Sans Serif, Inc.

This book is dedicated to "Angie" who passed away June 20, 1995. She has given me one of the greatest gifts I have ever received in my life—the gift of spiritual knowledge. If it had not been for her guidance and wisdom, this book would never have manifested. Because of her unselfish love, I am living a blessed, beautiful life. All who knew her felt her warmth, compassion and enthusiasm for others. Her presence is always near those she loves.

She is truly an Angel.

Contents

CONTENTS

Chapter Twelve
*An easy step-by-step formula to help you
predict the next nine years of your love life!*

Chapter Thirteen

Chapter Fourteen

Chapter Fifteen
*Brief summaries of what the first ten years of the new millennium
holds in store for each of the twelve Zodiac signs*

Preface:
ABOUT THIS BOOK

I love spending hours in bookstores. For years, I have run right into the New Age and Religion sections. Years ago, there were just a few shelves of these special interest books. Within the past five years, stores have had to expand their space and selections to satisfy readers with a hunger for spiritual knowledge.

Over the years, I have counseled thousands of people about their future paths and relationships. It seemed that the same questions came up again and again. Everyone wanted to know about past lives, karma, soul mates and who their "perfect partner" showed to be in their astrology chart.

Rather than writing ten different books on all of these topics, I have chosen to include knowledge about many of these areas in one book.

You may find my book a handy reference "love guide." Others may use it to learn to meditate or perhaps find the right healing crystal.

The general idea behind this book is to help you gain more understanding about how to work on yourself and better your relationships.

Heart and Soul is the type of book that has a little bit of everything in it to help us understand some of the mysteries and magic of love.

Acknowledgments

I would like to thank my husband David and daughters Jana and Sierra for their support while writing this book. Special thanks to my editor Cy Leder, Professor Emmeritus, Journalism and English, all of my true friends who shared their wisdom, stories and experiences for this effort. To March Walker for introducing me to 3 in 1 Concepts. Matthew Weatherford, for his computer savvy. To my parents for their unconditional love. All of the wonderful ladies and gentlemen I have worked with at our fairs and seminars. To the many clients, I consider all of them, friends, on a spiritual path. Most of all to God and the power of His Love.

CHAPTER ONE

Spiritual Love

I am writing this book out of love. Love for all of those hearts who give so freely. For people who have loved and lost, time and time again. For the romantics who don't let memories die. For the soul mates who have found one another and those still searching.

Love is like air. We need it to survive. Without love, our lives are empty, lonely and incomplete. It really doesn't matter what kind of love it is, as long as we can feel it and allow our hearts to breathe it in. It can be as simple as love between two friends or as strong as the unconditional love of a mother for her child.

In my private practice, I have counseled thousands and thousands of people all over the world. An overwhelmingly majority of my clients ask about romantic love.

When we were children, we fantasized about who we'd fall in love with. Happily-ever-after fairy tales provided us with a picture of what love was supposed to be like. Little girls dream of their marrying their handsome prince. Little boys long to be the knight in shinning armor slaying the dragons for their princess.

The older we get, the more we realize fairytales aren't real. Love like that doesn't exist. Or does it? Deep down, we still hold hope and we search endlessly until we find that special someone.

Being in love can bring many emotions; joy, compassion, kindness and even fear. Fear, because once we have found something so wonderful, we fear to lose it. This is where jealousy, control and manipulation can rear their ugly heads in a loving relationship.

To better understand how to deal with these overpowering emotions, we need to work on our spiritual sides. A spiritually healthy individual will find no reason to fear. They will trust their heart that the love they give will be received and returned. In today's society, every couple shares baggage from previous relationships. Some share heavy karma, which I will discuss in-depth in another chapter.

I tell my clients, there's something to learn from every relationship. No relationship is a waste of time. The most frustrating relationships are the ones that offer the most growth. We learn from experience. People learn more from crisis and pain rather than joy and success. I am not suggesting anyone stay in a bad or abusive relationship. But if we do find ourselves in a negative relationship, we should look at it as a learning experience and move on. We should grow from it.

Contrary to popular belief, we do not draw lovers for our personal growth. We draw partners for our soul's growth. Our ego tells us we feel good when we are with that special someone. We think marriage will help us keep that special feeling. Love has nothing to do with our personalities or our egos. Our ego or personality is what first attracts us to one another. But on a deeper level, it's our soul that knows what we need. It makes the connection with that we call "true love".

Ever hear the expression, "He captured my soul"? Our souls connect with another's for the sake of learning, growing and loving. Therefore, it is important that both partners work to build the spiritual side of their relationship. They do that by placing their egos aside and making compassion, kindness and unconditional love a priority. A spiritual relationship has no room for jealousy or betrayal. I tell my clients, "You are a reflection of your partner's soul. We are mirrors of one another. What you lack or what your soul needs, it will draw to you, to fill itself. Your partner's soul needs what you have." That's why opposites attract. When we fail to allow our higher selves to take over, we end up despising the very things that drew us to one another in the first place.

For example, my client Sheri was very attracted to Paul because he seemed so self-assured and in control. He was always cool and collected. Paul was drawn to Sheri for her sensitive emotional side. She could express her feelings freely. As the relationship progressed, Sheri grew tired of Paul's "cocky" attitude. He never seemed to show any emotions toward her. She hated that he could be so distant. Paul was starting to tire of Sheri's emotional mood swings. He became easily irritated when she wanted to talk about their relationship.

When scenarios like this take over, we know our souls are not growing. Our personalities are taking over and our egos are kicking in. If we veer too far off our spiritual path, the relationship will end.

My client, Tina, is a good example of understanding how the spiritual side of love works. She had to let go of her ego's needs first in order to achieve what was best for her heart and soul.

Tina and her boyfriend Tim had a terrible breakup. She caught him with another woman. What Tina didn't know at the time was that Tim also had another girlfriend who just had his baby. Two weeks after the devastating breakup, Tina learned she too was pregnant with Tim's child.

But Tim wanted nothing to do with her. He moved in with woman number three. For months Tina cried day and night. She would not let go of her love for Tim. She was determined to win him back. Her pleas didn't work and her heart was truly broken. She miscarried a week later. Unable to forget Tim, Tina took action. She still loved him despite what he'd done to her. Because she couldn't reach Tim on a physical level, (he refused to see her), she decided to speak to his soul. She started praying. She sent loving thoughts his way. She wrote positive affirmations every morning and night. She asked God to help her become a better person and to understand why Tim hurt her so deeply.

Tina started believing in her heart that things would work out for the best. She had faith the universe would bring back the love she so desperately needed. Two months went by, Tim called to see how she was doing. She was so excited! But the thrill didn't last. He was still with the other woman.

Tina started saying Saint Jude novenas, asking for just one more chance with Tim. She prayed unselfishly for Tim to prosper and be happy. Everyday, she did her meditations and continued her affirmations. They were now a part of her daily routine. She noticed she wasn't crying anymore. Nine months passed. It was rumored Tim was engaged. But Tina didn't give up. Her friends told her she was crazy.

It was shortly afterwards that the universe responded to Tina's requests for love. But not how you would think. The power of the universe is great. When Tina gave up the tears and pampering her wounded ego, she was able to put the problem in God's hand. She sent out positive energy through her affirmations and prayer.

On a cold, winter morning, Tina had to go to the market to get milk for breakfast. She really didn't want to go. She delayed going, making excuses all the while but something kept telling her she'd better go.

As she pulled into the supermarket parking lot, a tall dark-haired man pulled in. She was shaking. It was Tim! On second glance, the man looked like Tim but surely wasn't.

He was the same height, about the same weight and had the same warm smile. But something about this man was dif-· ferent. They were immediately attracted to one another. They went for coffee. She asked him his name. I am not kidding— his name was Tim! But this Tim was different. He was an honest, down-to-earth settled soul. The kind of Tim, Tina had been visualizing and praying for. After two years of courtship, the couple married and had a son. "I am happier than I ever thought I could be!" Tina tells me. "I am so glad I didn't end up with the other Tim."

The universe heard Tina's requests. It didn't give her what she wanted. It sent what she needed. It considered the soul. She was rewarded for her faith and trust. It sent her true love.

No relationship is ever going to be perfect. There will always be ups and downs and twist and turns to deal with. But if one person is putting their heart and soul into a relationship, and the other works only off ego issues, the relationship will be very difficult to maintain. It is then up to the enlightened partner to know when to walk away. They must accept the fact that the ego-driven lover will not permit the relationship to be a spiritual one.

For their own growth and ultimate happiness they must leave or accept the other person totally, without trying to change them. Sometimes by leaving, the ego-driven partner is forced to deal with their fear and pain. (Remember, we learn more through experiencing pain and sorrow than any other emotion). In some cases, the person learns and grows from the experience and the couple may reunite. Many times, they do not. Walls have been built up over the years through past mistrusts and betrayals.

The best thing people can do to better a relationship is to work on themselves first. You have to be healthy before you can draw a healthy relationship to you.

If you're not spiritually developed, you will continue to draw challenging mates with heavy issues. This basically means you need to be enlightened.

Acceptance also plays a big part in the success of relationships. I do not mean just accepting the other person, but accepting who you are is equally important. If you like yourself, other people will like you. It's that's simple. If you accept yourself, you will draw others' acceptance.

People work like magnets. We draw things, sometimes unknowingly, to ourselves. So when a client says to me, "The only kind of men I draw are jerks!" they are putting that thought out into the universe. They will undoubtedly continue to draw undesirables because they believe in that thought. They accept that ideal.

Everyone has a self-image of themselves, what they believe to be true. We get our self-image from our parents, our teachers, our friends and these days, the media influences how we think of ourselves.

Growing up, if we were told we were smart, we did well in school. If a little girl was told she was pretty, she felt pretty, acted pretty and therefore others saw her confidence in her looks and she was admired. If children were abused or told they were stupid, they felt insecure, and unworthy of being loved. We project what we think we are. What we've been conditioned to believe about ourselves since birth is how we act. Then when we grow up, we carry these self-images to the outside world and into relationships. If someone's self-image is poor, they will not fare well in any type of relationship. People definitely need to work on themselves before a healthy relationship with someone can materialize.

Knowledge is power. Understanding why you feel the way you do and the conditions in your upbringing are important in order to know what to change. Once you do, you can work on those issues, perhaps through therapy. When you no longer expect failure, you can't manifest it.

Another wonderful way to create more acceptance and become more fulfilled from a soul perspective is to understand the true meaning of why you are here and your life's purpose. Once you are fulfilled, you won't need a partner to fulfill you and therefore will only accept, chose and draw healthy people to you.

CHAPTER TWO

Your Soul's Purpose

For some people, their purpose in life is to lend support. For a number of folks, it is to teach. Others are here to heal. Some are here to share with the world their talents for music or writing. There are people who fulfill a purpose in a big way, like Princess Diana and Mother Teresa. Their efforts affected the entire world. Yet others humbly serve mankind without any appreciation or recognition at all. Most of us touch just a few people's lives. Whether we reach out to the masses or make a difference in just one person's life, all types of service are equally important.

Learn the difference between ego and soul. Decide if you are doing something in your life out of a need to get recognition, appreciation or attention. Or if you are working off an unselfish desire to help people. The basic reason we are all here on this earth plane is to be of service to others. We are not here to see how much money we can make or how famous we will become. That is an ego-driven existence.

The basis for our being is love. The more love we put out into the universe, the more we get back. If we are on the right path, things come very easily. If we encounter obstacle after obstacle and things never go right in our lives, this is a good indicator we are not on the right road. It is time to examine what we really should be doing.

If more people realized this, we would have better relationships, functioning families and more peace in the world. If everyone followed this direction, prejudice and hatred would be a thing of the past. One person alone may not be able to change the entire world, but if you can change yourself, you will change your relationships for the better.

My own personal story is a case in point. For fifteen years I worked in the entertainment field. I was looking to fill a void in my heart. I was given up for adoption at six months old and thus had a subconscious need for approval and love. Even though I enjoyed a loving childhood, the pain of being given away made me feel unworthy or not good enough.

So, at an early age I decided to be famous. I loved to write and told everyone I was going to a great journalist one day. I did pretty well. From age sixteen to age thirty, I worked in newspaper, radio and television fields. I hosted my own television talk show, did morning-drive radio and was the editor of a national magazine. I still did not feel fulfilled or successful, but my friends were envious. They thought I had the most glamorous life; dating celebrities, going to the best parties and being on television. But I never truly felt fulfilled. It wasn't easy to maintain the pace. The excitement of the career wore thin. I had to work so hard just to maintain the success level I had reached, that it didn't seem worth it. I worked long hours and didn't feel the rewards.

The entertainment business is cut throat. You are at the mercy of the executive producer, the news director, or the magazine publisher. I remember back in 1985, I moved away, left my family and friends, and took a huge pay cut to accept a position at a major magazine. The job title was most impressive. Celebrities were clamoring to get a mention in my magazine. After making my way to the top, the everyday stress was unbearable and the publisher came in nine months later and fired the entire staff. I loved the media business at times, and there were times I hated it.

I was desperately trying to find security in a career world that offered none.

The turning point for me came one day when my husband uprooted the family to further his career. I was forced to quit my job and find new employment. When I couldn't find work in my field, I grew depressed.

My ego was hurt and I felt nothing but rejection. I knew I was good: My talents and gifts were stronger than many others that were in the positions I sought. No matter how much effort I put out, nothing came back. I am a very determined person. But the universe knew what was best for me. I was forced into a brand new direction.

I began studying metaphysical topics. They fascinated me and I was soon learning all about the science of astrology that I could. Teachers appeared in my life offering help and guidance. It is said that when the student is ready, the teacher appears. I was ready. I started a small astrological counseling service and hundreds of people were drawn to me, many by word of mouth. My income was climbing. Within a year, I was in an entirely new business and a whole new world had opened up to me.

My financial picture grew bigger and brighter than I could ever hope. I put in long hours but they didn't seem like work. I was helping dozens of people every week understand their spiritual path, helping them find the answers within them to solve problems and give them hope for their future. I was sharing my love and compassion with complete strangers. People were loving me back. I grew so much emotionally. Rude remarks didn't hurt my feelings like they used too. If something negative happened, I looked for the positive in it.

Yet, back then and to this day, I do not feel what I do is a job. It is not even a career. It is a life path. I feel as if I am helping friends in need. I share my knowledge, visions and ideas. I have found my spiritual path. Things come easy in my life. I have no desire to cover the latest breaking story on network news any more.

I never worry about where I'll be in five years and my relationships are better. I do not feel ego-driven. I get fulfillment when clients call and tell me that I have made a difference in their lives or I've helped them through a difficult time. It doesn't matter if one person knows my name or a thousand. But I will tell you that I have met more wonderful people in the first two years of my spiritual work than in my fifteen years of broadcasting. I know I have touched more people's lives in a meaningful way, and they in turn, have touched mine. I feel alive and I feel loved.

The difference between my two walks of life is clear: The media field was ego-driven. There was always stress, fear or insecurity. Walking my spiritual path, I feel in control and safe and I know I don't have to worry anymore. The universe supplies my every need.

In relationships, ego needs are always different from the soul's. The ego looks to getting its own needs met over anything else. It needs superiority. The soul's need is fulfillment, which requires delays in immediate gratification. It often means helping others before helping itself.

Many people do not find there's a balance in their relationships. One partner is usually battling their fearful ego. Once they achieve a certain status in the relationship, they strive to maintain it and fight change.

People coming from this position, are thinking of their selves. They feel if they give of themselves too much, they are being used or abused.

They look only at how much they can benefit from the union. Without changing these patterns, the couple stop growing together and the universe stops working for them.

If both partners have found their own spiritual path, they will grow together. To find your path, it is good to use the talents you were born with. I use my communication abilities to counsel those in need. If you write, write a book or article that will help readers in some way. If you have a skill, pass it on by teaching it to someone else. If you have lots of love to give, become a parent. Being a good parent is one of the best ways you can achieve soul fulfillment.

If you devote your life to being of service to others, for the sake of their betterment and not your own, the universe will reward you generously. All of your emotional, physical and material needs will be taken care of. There will be no reason for stress or worry.

My prayer is that everyone who is reading this book will take the time to find their spiritual path and allow it to open up for them. Not only will your own life be more fulfilling but the relationships around you will benefit. We all need love to survive. If we truly open our hearts and our souls to the possibilities, we can all live rich, long and loving lives.

CHAPTER THREE

Your Life's Path and Lessons

Each sign of the zodiac has special talents. If you aren't already aware of what your talents are, the following information may help you on the road to finding your own special path for service and ultimately spiritual growth. Each sign also has special challenges to overcome in relationships. These are also discussed over the next pages.

Aries

Aries have been given strong sharp minds. They would do well to use their gifts in areas of teaching, counseling, supervising and managing. They can use their fighting spirit to stand up for causes and the rights of others.

In love, they should work on putting their partner's needs ahead of their own. They should strive for more of a balance in a marriage or commitment. Aries need to set the ego aside and let their heart speak.

Taurus

Taurus are blessed with artistic talent. Many have beautiful voices. They could excel in areas of singing, acting, artistry or dance. It is important they share these gifts with the universe. Taurus also have been given a good business and financial sense. They could help others managing money or with investing.

Taurus need to trust the love they give, will come back to them. They should not fear loss but be open to change. Release the need to possess, Taurus, and learn that security comes from within.

Gemini

Gemini have been given the gift of gab. They are the communicators of the zodiac. It is important they channel these gifts into areas of teaching, writing, counseling and perhaps working with children. Gemini needs to experience a variety of relationships and emotions before making a commitment. Learn to create strong communication in love.

Cancer

Cancer is the sign of the mother. They were born with a natural desire to nurture people. They have compassion and are very psychic. They do well in parenting roles, as ministers, day care providers, family counselors and as homemakers.

Cancer's challenge in love is to let go of the past and move on. Feel more self-assured and deserving of love. Cancer, you do not need to smother loved ones to receive the appreciation and security you desire. Be more trusting of the universe to bring you the love you need.

Leo

Leo was given a talent for entertaining. They have a great sense of humor and much creativity. Leos make great actors, broadcasters, and musicians. Any type of business in which they can express creativity and love works well. Many are fine leaders and entrepreneurs.

Leo's ego needs to be set aside so their generous hearts can shine. Know that you can manifest whatever it is you truly desire. Don't be afraid to wear your heart on your sleeve.

Virgo

Virgo have qualities which include dedication and unselfish service to others. They also have healing powers. They make excellent nurses, physicians and massage therapists, health care professionals and teachers.

Virgo's lesson in love is to be of service to others. Be open to giving but equally open to receiving love. Realize that the perfection you seek first comes from within.

Libra

Libra is a creative sign. They are born with a sense of honesty and fairness. Libra have an ability to see both sides of the coin. Many Libras do well working as lawyers, judges, marriage counselors and professional matchmakers.

In love, Libra's lesson is to create a peaceful and harmonious spirit first within them selves. Be open to the beauty and simple pleasures life and love have to offer.

Scorpio

Scorpio has a very deep psychological understanding of the universe. They have great healing powers and the ability to look at life and death in more spiritual terms than most people. They make great doctors, researchers, detectives, astrologers, grief counselors and hospice workers.

Scorpio needs not to confuse control with security in love. They need to learn to allow their emotions to come out and play and express those deep intense feelings with their partner.

Sagittarius

The Sagittarius are born with an understanding of higher philosophy and a yearning for spiritual knowledge. They are exceptional public speakers. Sagittarius make good politicians, lawyers, negotiators and international diplomats. With their natural athletic abilities, they make fine personal trainers and sports figures. Sagittarius' love lesson is a spiritual one. They need to look at love for what it is: a higher, more meaningful energy. They need to be honest and truthful with their own feelings.

Capricorn

Capricorn have business and organizational skills. They excel in management and business positions, overseers, police work, government and corporate careers. Capricorn needs to allow their emotional side to show, to be less cautious in opening their heart and have more faith in what the universe can bring them.

Aquarius

Aquarius are here to make the world a better place. They have humanitarian natures and possess a sense of fairness. They make excellent social reformers, fund-raisers, politicians, scientists, environmentalists and evangelists. Aquarius should love the world, express their true feelings more and work on detachment issues.

Pisces

Pisces have the ability to dream and to be very creative. They are psychic and would work well in any type of field where they are helping others. Many Pisces own hair salons, service businesses and retail shops. Many are quite wealthy because of their own business endeavors.

Pisces need to trust their feelings. If they can accept themselves for what they really are, not what others want them to be, they will prosper in love. It is also important that Pisces choose emotionally healthy mates who do not capitalize on Pisces' sympathetic natures.

Spiritual Development Through Life Path

Many people define their Life Path as their career path. Ideally, you could combine the two.

Make a list of all of your talents and skills. See where they could fit into a career choice. Many successful professionals say what they do for a living, doesn't seem like work to them. These are people who have combined their life path with their careers.

They call what they do their "passion". Just as many people say they really don't know how to capture that passion. They aren't sure what it is they are suppose to be doing. Many just feel "stuck in a rut". Perhaps you can find your answers by taking different classes that interest you. You can also speed the discovery process along by doing affirmations and meditations. Everyone needs a little bit of time everyday to just sit and think. We are all so busy that we seldom take time to listen to our inner voice. That inner voice usually has all of our answers. We just need to listen.

It's a good idea to take the time to get in touch with your creative side too. Being creative stirs the juices. It makes you feel alive. Write. Sing. Dance. Draw. Doodle. Even cooking can be creative.

Learn to meditate. It will not only help you find answers within yourself but reduce your stress levels as well. It's much easier than you would think. The more you meditate, the more you will find it necessary and make time for it. If you are not sure how to meditate, I suggest getting a cassette tape that can help guide you through the process. You can find a wide assortment in the health or New Age areas of a bookstore. Many times your spirit guides will give you messages about your life path. Through meditation, you can link up to your higher self, and your subconscious will speak to you. You'll be surprised at how easily the thoughts will come.

Another way to find your life path or purpose is through your astrology or natal chart. Astrologers need your time of birth, the date you born and the city of your birth to make a chart. The chart resembles a wheel, made up of twelve sections (or houses). Each section signifies a part of your life. The planets in our solar system and where they were stationed at the time of your birth can give you specific information on your fate or destiny. Transiting planets predict opportunity and challenges to look for. There are three placements I look for in a natal chart to determine the life purpose: the nodes, the twelfth house in the chart and in which house the sun is placed. They are easy to recognize and fairly easy to interpret.

Many times astrologers can pinpoint exactly what the client's karma and soul's purpose is. If a person follows their chart, things flow easier. If a person neglects to understand and put the proper perspectives in their life, there are more challenges.

Astrology is like a roadmap of your life. You don't have to use your special map. You can ignore it for a while if you choose because you are in the driver's seat. But the more you veer off your path, the more roadblocks and collisions you'll run into. If you stick to it, life becomes a superhighway!

Most people also don't realize that we have chosen our life path before we were born. With a belief system which includes reincarnation, we all have predestined lives and there's something we are here to accomplish in our current lifetime for our soul's growth.

Of the thousands of charts I have interpreted over the years, the majority of people are here to experience growth through spiritual development, career, service or relationships. This leads me to the next chapter on karma in relationships. There are many people in this world who keep coming back, lifetime after lifetime, to work on love and commitment issues. Often these souls will get involved with the same people (souls) over and over again until they "get it right" and learn their love lessons.

CHAPTER FOUR

Karma

There are so many definitions of karma. Many are quite confusing. To make it simple: Whatever you put out comes back to you. For every action, there is a reaction. Whatever kindness you do, will come back to you three-fold. Likewise, any negative deeds will come back at you.

Karma teaches us lessons. If you fail or refuse to learn your lessons, karma will keep coming back until you learn. The purpose of karma is to move our souls to a higher level. The more we learn, the more we grow. When our egos take over and we refuse to learn or accept responsibility for our actions, we experience more lessons and hardships. These often become repetitive cycles.

It is important to remember that you are the only person responsible for your karma. Karma is the result of your own thoughts and deeds, not someone else's. If a person has unfinished business (karma) when they die, their soul is still in need of fulfilling its karma, or it can't advance to the next level of spiritual enlightenment. Therefore, when it reincarnates, it likely will experience karma from the previous lifetime. This is why past life regression and therapy is so important. It helps us understand, whether or not, the issues we deal with are of this lifetime or another.

Do you ever feel Deja Vu? Like you've met someone before or you've known them all of your life? Do your relationship scenarios feel frighteningly familiar? Do the same old issues come up in every new love encounter? I feel anyone that you have a strong bond with in this lifetime or have major issues with is likely to be a past life connection.

Sometimes when you first meet a person, you know right away there's some sort of connection between you both. With others, it may take a few "lessons" to figure it out. Remember, karma can be good or bad. It can carry over from several lifetimes. It is easier to deal with karma in your current lifetime, because it has a tendency to grow more difficult with each existence. Karma can also be a "promise" between two people to "make things right" or to "pay back a debt".

I have helped many people identify what their karma is over the years. Also I've been able to pinpoint exact people with whom they have past life or soul connections through their astrological charts. Here's an example of good karma concerning some close friends.

The New Orleans Nuns

Cindy and Angie had a strong past-life connection. Both being spiritually open to such ideals, they shared their feelings and beliefs with one another. When they first met in 1993, they felt an instant recognition and talked like old friends. They had a desire to find out where this connection came from. After a few meditation and past-life regressions sessions, the friends were able to narrow down the past life, which they shared. Both were Ursuline nuns who had been assigned to come over from France to New Orleans in the early 1800's. This would explain Cindy's draw to the historic French Quarter in this lifetime. She also has no desire to visit the former Ursuline Convent in the Quarter when she visits. She claims her stomach gets upset just crossing the street on which it sits.

Back then, nuns were brought over from France to educate and bring religion to the city, which was infested with greed, gambling, piracy and other goings on. Every time Cindy visits New Orleans, she has terribly vivid dreams depicting life a century or so ago. Many people she knows today show up in these dreams. She has often shared these dreams with me, and they are very descriptive. It seems being in New Orleans, her subconscious is opening itself up to another time in which she lived. This must have been a significant lifetime for her because she remembers names, faces and buildings. Some of the sites she describes can still be found in the Quarter today.

After doing more research and meditation, Cindy and Angie agreed that they had been very close friends. During this prior lifetime, Cindy had fallen sick from the yellow fever epidemic. Angie had been at Cindy's deathbed around the clock. She was taking care of her during her final days and helping guide her into the afterlife. Cindy made a promise then. She vowed that she would be with Angie to help her through her transition in the next lifetime.

This came to pass. Shortly after they had met in 1993, Angie was dying of breast cancer. Families and friends had been there everyday for six months as her condition worsened. Out of the blue, Cindy left her own family and quit her job to come sit at Angie's bedside. She was there twenty-four hours a day, seven days week, nursing her and talking with her.

Family came in and out but Cindy stayed. Three weeks later, Angie was ready to leave the earth plane. Cindy was right there, holding her hand as she took her final breath . . . just as she had promised to, in the lifetime they shared over 150 years ago.

Angie laid good karma in the New Orleans lifetime by helping her friend on her final journey. Cindy repaid that karmic debt by doing the same lifetimes later. To this day, Cindy says she doesn't really know why she chose to drop everything and take care of Angie even though Angie had nurses and family there for her. She said it was just the right thing to do. "It was just natural. I knew I was the one supposed to be there. It was something I had to do. Nothing else in the world mattered," she recalled.

These two friends recognized their connection early on in their relationship, but they didn't recognize what their karma was or what debt was to be paid until the end of the relationship.

Repetitive Patterns

Mickey and Sharly share a different story. Their karma is not easy to define. No matter how hard they try to work out issues or end their turbulent relationship, it doesn't happen. During a past-life session, we were able to discover Mickey was in love with Sharly who had talent to make it big in the music industry as a singer.

But Mickey wanted to control Sharly and was jealous of any success that might take her away from him. The two became co-dependent on one another. Their lifestyle contributed to their drug and alcohol abuse.

In this prior lifetime, Sharly eventually died of a drug overdose, never realizing her dreams of becoming famous. Mickey never married and for years after her death was a recluse.

In this lifetime, these two met and instantly fell in love. The attraction was so intense that they both felt it and became inseparable. On their first date they started arguing over silly little things and fell into co-dependent patterns.

Ironically, both of these people had an interest in acting and singing in this lifetime. They both felt they would have to accomplish their individual goals before they could marry, and worked hard on their careers. During the course of their relationship, they were constantly breaking up and getting back together. Sharly never trusted Mickey. She couldn't explain these unfounded feelings. She told me she had never loved anyone so strongly before but she knew the relationship wasn't good for her. She also was angry with Mickey although he did nothing to provoke her. On numerous occasions, she would cheat on him. When she did, she always felt vindicated. Bad patterns were constantly being repeated year after year in the relationship.

Finally Sharly came to me for past-life counseling sessions. We began the long, hard journey of releasing her karma from the previous lifetime so she could get on with this one. These two had heavy karma to deal with. I was sure they had experienced many similar lifetimes together. In each lifetime their problems persisted and grew stronger. Obsession, control, and anger issues came up in all regression sessions.

Somewhere in their subconscious, these two knew they had to make this relationship right, to turn it around and stop the insanity. That was why it was so difficult to end the relationship for good. There was so much unfinished karma. Because the couple wasn't aware of what really lay behind current conditions, they grew frustrated. Bad karma followed more bad karma as Mickey and Sharly continued hurting each other.

The reason Sharly didn't leave was that she couldn't. Until the couple finished their old karma or released it, both felt compelled to stay. They had debts to pay to each other. So Mickey continued to hurt Sharly and Sharly, in turn, hurt Mickey, and the karma went back and forth. Thus, there was no end in sight.

Once people like Mickey and Sharly are enlightened to the law of karma, they can repay their debts and release them.

CHAPTER FIVE

Releasing Karmic Debts

hen someone is spiritually enlightened, he or she does not need to be a keeper of bad karma forever. The chain can be broken at some point. Looking at the previous story between Mickey and Sharly, it was Sharly who was the "victim" in the former lifetime. Mickey had given her drugs and took control of her life, thus leading to her demise. Sharly doesn't know why she feels anger toward Mickey in their current lifetime. But at times, she wants to hurt him. It's as if she feels he deserves it.

When such anger comes over Sharly, she can stop herself and ask, "Why?" She needs to examine her real motivation for hurting Mickey. She can make a conscious decision to stop "trying to get back at him." If she can do this every time she feels the urge to use or hurt him, she is saying "No" to karmic retribution, thus breaking patterns set over lifetimes. She is also avoiding retribution coming back to her in this lifetime or the next from Mickey. This is not always easy to do, especially if we are working from the ego level.

Now let's look at breaking karmic patterns from the other way around. I'll suggest that Sharly doesn't believe in karma in this current lifetime but Mickey does. Mickey understands the pain he put Sharly through in a former life. He may even accept and acknowledge it. Once Mickey accepts the debt and holds no resentment for Sharly's current anger, he can forgive her. He will not fight back but does all he can to bring peace to the situation. Mickey is handling his karmic responsibilities correctly. In the next lifetime, the pattern will not be repeated and it's likely the karmic debt will be paid in full.

There is another concept I have discovered in the past several years for releasing karma from prior lifetimes. It is called 3 in 1 Concepts. It is a form of stress diffusion that gets right to the root of problems and is emerging as a great tool in helping people with all sorts of issues, not just those from prior lifetimes, but current conditions as well. Many of our current conditions may be rooted in past lifetimes.

Each time we are born into a new lifetime, our soul still retains a "memory" of our previous incarnation but our conscious mind does not. So therefore experiences, fears, talents, traumas and the like are engraved in genetic cells, our subconscious mind and soul recall. By using age-recession and generation-recession techniques, clients can be gently guided back to the thoughts and emotions of a prior lifetime.

The facilitators, using 3-in-1 suggested remedies, (Bach flower, essences, affirmations, balancing, color therapy), make corrections to the clients' subconscious, conscious and physical states in current times. Negative energy and thoughts are then released, and in turn, some karmic patterns are immediately halted.

Your karma with someone doesn't mean you must be with that person forever. The role you play in the relationship may last for a short while, but have eternal rewards.

Perhaps the worst thing about karmic debt is that we don't remember what it is we are paying for. Whatever our debt was we brought over from a prior lifetime, we have no conscious memory of it.

Therefore, past-life regression, meditation, astrological study and spiritual awareness are essential in breaking or healing the karma debts and restitutions from our past.

CHAPTER SIX

Karmic Paybacks

K armic repayments happen to all of us everyday. You need to be aware and accepting of them. Let's say something negative happens to you at work. You should stop and think, "What have I done recently to afford this? Did I mistreat someone yesterday, a week ago, a year ago?"

Whatever you put out comes back to you. Even thoughts are like boomerangs. Put out a negative thought, you'll get it back. If you think you can achieve something, you will. How many times do we get up in the morning and say "It's going to a rotten day"? Then the next twenty-four hours of your life turns out to be exactly that.

However you want to be treated, you must treat others. If you want to be understood, you must listen. If you want respect, you must give it. If you want love, you must open your heart to it.

People born under the sign of Scorpio have a very special

type of karma. It is called Kash-Karma. Kash-Karma brings immediate paybacks for good or bad deeds in this lifetime. This sign doesn't have to wait until another lifetime to get theirs!

I'll never forget my best buddy Dan, a Scorpio. He was such a character. We were about eighteen years old at the time when he invited me out to a very nice dinner one evening. When the bill came, he told me to go ahead to the ladies room and he'd meet me in the outside lobby.

I did as he suggested and found him with an anxious look on this face. "C'mon," he whispered, "let's get out of here." I ran after him questioning his rush. "I'll tell you in the car," he said. As he wheeled out of the parking lot, he was laughing. "I skipped out on the bill!" he said. "We got a free dinner!" We only drove about two miles when we saw a police officer sitting on the side of the road. He immediately flashed us over. The officer said Dan was speeding 30 miles over the speed limit. We both knew he wasn't. The officer handed him a ticket and told him he could fight it in court. Our $70 dinner was ruined.

The court date was set for Dan to challenge the ticket. I was to be a witness for him. We went to court, we lost, and Dan had to pay a fine of $70. Even though I was an unknowing accomplice in Dan's plan, it so happened the court date was set on my birthday and I had to spend the entire day in a small county courthouse, waiting our turn to be heard. To make matters worse, I took the day off from work without pay. All of this would never have happened if we had just paid the dinner bill.

This is an example of the way the universe works in paying us back the karma we owe. If you think you're getting away with something, you'll end up paying in the long run!

Just think of all of the people who seem to be getting away with bad deeds. There are those people who think they will never get caught. Their debts are mounting with the universe keeping score. Karma will catch up to them sooner or later and their paybacks will be something else!

I also remember when I had my purse stolen in a locker room years ago. I was devastated. I had just cashed my payroll check. All the money for the next few weeks was in the purse, plus a 35mm camera and, of course, all of my identification. The police were called and said there was nothing they could do. "How could this happen to such a nice person like me?" I moaned. "What had I done to deserve this?" I hadn't ripped anyone off. Almost a week later, I received a raise where I worked, I got free tickets to a sold-out concert and I won a weeklong trip to Tennessee. I was rewarded three-fold by the universe for what had been taken from me. I often wondered what happened to the purse thieves!

Most recently, a friend who owns a retail store was at another department store. She took five dresses up to the cashier. The cashier forgot to ring one up, so my friend didn't say anything and figured she got a free dress.

A week later one of her own customers used a stolen

credit card. The fraud cost her $240. The dress she got for "free" was only $39.95. She learned an expensive karmic lesson!

Heavier karma is usually found in relationships than in our everyday lives. I never judge anyone. I have clients from all walks of life and on their own path, learning what they need to learn. But my heart goes out to those people who have extra-martial affairs. Most are unaware of the karma they are creating. A client of mine, Chris, was involved with a married man. His wife was pregnant but Chris thought she was in love and stayed with this man for two years, encouraging the relationship. Chris was not laying good karma. She eventually married someone else, settled down and had two beautiful little girls. Seven years into the marriage, Chris' husband was caught having an affair. She fought to keep the marriage but the other woman was relentless in her pursuit. Chris and her husband got a divorce.

Seldom do I see happy endings when relationships start out of an illicit affair. Everyone ends up getting hurt sooner or later. This "other" woman married Chris's husband and is desperately trying to have a child. The last time I spoke with her, the doctors told the woman her chances of conception were zero. This woman fears her new husband will never be as close to her as he once was with Chris. She is going to therapy to overcome those fears.

Meanwhile, Chris understands how the law of karma worked for her and others, even years later.

I deal with so many affairs in my practice. These are the most difficult situations. There are a few exceptions in which all seems to turn out okay, but seldom do I see good things. There is bad karma for years. I usually advise couples in the affairs to step back and allow a marriage the time it needs to rebuild itself or end. If it fails, then after the divorce they can start a relationship. You can save yourself a lot of pain and bad karma by just stepping back. You can also earn yourself good karma in the meantime.

Situations like we've discussed in the past pages occur everyday. If people realized that for every thought or action, they are sending out to the universe, it will come back to them, this world would run a lot smoother. But until the law of karma is learned and accepted by everyone, the debts keep mounting.

CHAPTER SEVEN

Paying Off Karmic Debt

ou can pay off your debt if you know what your karma is. One of the most common karmic debts I have found among my clients concerns children. I get calls from women desperate to have children. Their doctors give them little or no hope.

Even in-vitro fertilization doesn't work in some of these cases. In these situations, I always look to the astrological chart of the individual and their mates to see where the karmic responsibility lies. More than likely, present conditions have to do with a past lifetime of not wanting children or being neglectful to the ones they did have. Since the couple has no recollection of such a past life, they can't understand why such good loving people shouldn't be blessed with children.

Often if the woman or man performs some sort of

service in their current lifetime to children such as working with abused kids or even adopting them, the karma is paid back and they conceive almost immediately.

How many times have you heard as soon as a woman adopts a child, she becomes pregnant? Happens all the time. This is a good example of balancing your karma.

Many people are born with handicaps or experience health troubles. Many bring these issues over from a former lifetime. A Michigan man had a previous lifetime in which he was a solider killed in war. During a past life-regression session he saw himself in uniform, something like that of a union soldier in the Civil War. He knew he didn't want to fight. He was forced to join the army and was killed as a result of a battle. In this lifetime, he reincarnated with a health problem that made him unable to be eligible for any kind of military service.

The health problems came up around his 18th birthday. His soul made sure he wouldn't be eligible for any draft in this lifetime. It's amazing that the illness uncovered was related to the area of the body in which he was shot in the Civil War. During a regression, he saw himself being shot in the head, and in this lifetime, he was diagnosed with a mental illness. He undoubtedly had heavy karma in that other lifetime. He paid back his debt then by giving his life. His slate was wiped clean. So in this lifetime, he is being rewarded.

Rewarded? Yes. He will never have to fight in a war and he is still able to live a comfortable lifestyle. His illness is under control with medication and all of his needs are taken care of.

Many people wonder why babies are born with defects or why anyone would want to be born blind or crippled. These souls could be choosing to atone for their past actions in another lifetime. Their souls have chosen this path and are more than accepting. Sometimes people with handicaps, who do not have to atone for their actions from a previous lifetime, choose their current situation to help bring understanding to their families or friends for their soul's growth.

I will never forget as long as I live, the devastating and true story my father told me one day. When he was a young boy, there had been a neighbor boy who was quite mischievous. The boy was walking in the woods one day and caught a crow. He took out his jack-knife and cut the crow's eyes out. He let the crow go, wandering blindly, living the rest of its days in the dark woods. The boy was bragging about what he had done for weeks afterwards. I thought this the cruelest and most inhumane act I had ever heard of. But the story is not over. When the young boy grew up, he married and was expecting a child. When the baby finally arrived, it was born without eyes. There were holes in the eye sockets. To this day, that story has made an impact on me and sends chills up my spine.

This a perfect example of an unselfish soul coming down from Heaven to teach its father a lesson. It took years for the karma to come back, but when it did, it hit hard.

There is a reason for everything. God's plan is grand. Ultimately, our goal is for our soul to reach the highest level of spiritual enlightenment it possibly can.

Then what do we make of murderers, con artists, child molesters and people who rape and steal? Why do they do what they do? All of us are on a journey to get to that highest spiritual place. The choices we make allow some of us to reach that level sooner than others.

God has given us power of free will, the power to make our own choices. Some choices are obviously better than others. Many times, the younger souls are the ones that do not have the understanding. The younger the soul, the more lessons there are to learn. Sometimes the lessons are much harder than those that older souls choose to deal with.

Some older souls don't always have to reincarnate. They reach a certain level of understanding and enlightenment so it's really not necessary to come back. But those who do choose to return to the earth plane, are often here for a higher purpose. Among them you will recognize your spiritual leaders, researchers, teachers and healers. Many are found living their lives in humble service to others. They never seem to complain no matter what hardships they endure. That's because they know exactly what they are meant to do with their lives. Sometimes they come back just to help younger souls on their journey. A loss of a child at an early age can sometimes be explained under this theory.

I remember a client of mine, who had two children; an

eight-year-old daughter and a fifteen-year-old son. The brother and sister were extremely close. They loved one another more than most siblings, and the boy always took time to do things with his sister.

He died one day in a terrible accident. The mother came to see me, grief-stricken and could not understand why this could happen, why her son's life was cut short. After heavy meditation and prayer, I was able to understand and express exactly what had happened. I knew the message I received was the right one. I cried along with this mother as I expressed what spirit had allowed me to feel.

The son has finished his karma or lesson here on earth. The brother and sister's souls' agreement was simple: he was to help her through some difficult, early years while their parents were going through a divorce. By doing this, it also helped him achieve his purpose, which was to learn to love unselfishly. He completed his soul's lesson and then returned home to Heaven.

The mother and I accepted this message because it felt so right. We both knew that we had received a special gift of "knowing" from God.

The little sister told her mother that after her brother's death, he often spoke to her. She would hear his voice at times. Their bond had still not been broken.

Children, unlike most adults, do have a strong bond to the "other side". Their minds have not been filled with suspicions or negativity like adults. Therefore, they are open to feelings and the vibrations of loved ones who have passed on. Children, especially under the age of seven, have not turned over that special intuitive and spiritual side they possess, to the mundane world. Thus, they have the abilities to communicate easier with the souls of those they love. That's why so many children have experiences of visitations from their deceased loved ones. Adults sometimes pass this off as overactive imagination. Most children are not lying when they express these coincidences and should not feel afraid to do so.

In order to understand how to work on issues of loss and sadness, past-life regression and meditation can be helpful. Trusting your own heart is always the way to go. All of us are intuitive beings. The more we trust our inner feelings, the more they will work for us, to help us. You can call this mother's intuition, gut feeling or psychic ability. Whatever you call it, it works. Sometimes you will know who is calling when the telephone rings. Sometimes you'll be at the right place at the right time for a job offer or to meet that special someone.

Trust your intuition. It won't serve you wrong. Trust your feelings about someone. Your soul won't deceive you. Your head may play games with your heart. But your soul doesn't lie. If you know something to be true, you will experience overwhelming emotion. If you suddenly meet a stranger who seems like a dear old friend, this is truth. If you are so mesmerized by a beautiful sunset that it brings tears to your eyes, this is truth. Anything or anyone that affects you in such a strong, positive, powerful way, is truth.

Truth gives positive energy to our emotions. Meeting someone who triggers these emotions in our heart just may turn out to be a soul mate.

CHAPTER EIGHT

Soul Mates &
Karmic Marriage

The topic of soul mates comes up often when I am counseling clients on relationships. Almost everyone asks the question, "When will I meet my soul mate?" I feel the word is used too loosely these days.

Many times when people are in a wonderful relationship, they tend to think they've found their elusive soul mate. People who feel this way describe a deep soul-stirring emotion. They've been in love before, but nothing like this. They feel no jealousy, no fear and no threats to the relationship. They feel at peace and complete. Yes, there is a strong possibility they have found a soul mate. But there are many different types of soul mates and they do not necessarily have to be lovers, spouses or romantic interests. Many can be friends, neighbors, children and family members.

Soul mates come together because they are working on

the same type of karma in this lifetime. On their spiritual paths, they are drawn to one another because they feel such a strong connection. The feeling is not one of infatuation or obsession. It is peace. It is recognizing the fact that you are supposed to be with this other soul, for a higher purpose. Sometimes you will recognize what this higher purpose is; others times you have no clue, but you feel the relationship has a deep spiritual quality to it, like no other you have experienced before.

Many times it is possible to determine, through your astrological chart, the presence of a soul mate in your life or when one is coming. Once you've found your soul mate, it is important to know, that you may not choose to be together during an entire lifetime. Many soul mates stay together till death do them part, and many part ways once their karma has been completed.

Still many people never meet their soul mates. This is not a bad thing. It's just that their soul is choosing to walk its path alone. That is their karma.

A Soul-Stirring Experience

I recall a client from New York who had an interesting experience when she discovered her soul mate. For months, June had been having the same dreams at night. In the dreams, she was always meeting a particular man in a strange bar. She described this man in great detail, what he was wearing, his mannerisms, his eyes. She told me she felt as if her dream was trying to tell her something. When she was on a business trip out of state, she went into a bar, and before her stood this very man!

She was speechless. She felt a strong connection to his man. She remembered his eyes (the eyes are the windows of the soul). What did all of this mean? Was this her soul mate? The man also was from out of town and came into the bar lost and looking for help with directions. When he saw June, his mouth dropped. He told her he had been having dreams about her during the past few weeks. Before the evening was over, June dropped her boyfriend of two years. The new couple made plans to move in together and get married. The relationship was very intense.

Everything just fell into place for these lovers. I do not know what happened to June and her soul mate. I haven't heard from her since. But a meeting such as theirs only happens once in a lifetime, if at all. Their dreams were definitely their subconscious alerting them to expect a powerful encounter. The dreams helped them recognize each other so their souls would be guaranteed a chance to come together.

If you find your soul mate in this lifetime, it is important to find out what it is you are meant to be working on together. The relationship seems to fall in place pretty easily if you are aware of these responsibilities. Many times soul mates become marriage partners. If this is the case, there is another relationship at work here, called the "Karmic Marriage."

In such a marriage, there is mutual karma. Many times, these types of marriages are frustrating and difficult. If the husband and wife chose to have children and create a loving home environment, they are building good karma. Many of these unions offer souls a way to balance out karma from other lifetimes. Usually it is not good karma. There could have been previous betrayal, neglect, rape and even murder. By the two building a solid, nurturing home and family together, they are repaying the debt from a previous lifetime. These types of marriages are often the ones wrought with difficulties and disappointment but eventually lead to fulfillment.

You will hear many couples say "We've made it through hell and back." After all they've been through, they've earned good karma. Then they will experience the good life, a nice family, the dream home and financial security. We know marriage is hard work. A karmic marriage is the soul's work.

CHAPTER NINE

How Old of a Soul Are You?

H ow old is your soul? The age of the soul often reflects issues or challenges it has chosen to deal with in each lifetime. It is said that the younger the soul, the harder the lessons. As we pass through each lifetime, our souls grow closer to God. We are often helped or challenged by other souls along our path. In ego-based relationships, partners often feel controlled, manipulated or taken advantage of. If one person chooses not to work off the soul level, there is a rebellious undertone in the relationship.

I believe anyone can make any relationship work no matter how difficult it may be, if both partners are working on a soul level. If they willingly accept each other's path in life, there can be harmony. Even an old soul can learn to live with a young soul. Old souls are wiser, and young souls have much to learn from them. If they can accept their differences, they can learn much from one another.

You've heard the saying "A cat has nine lives." A very old concept handed down generation after generation suggests we, as humans, have nine lifetimes too. My deceased aunts taught me the formula years ago. It works!

My friend and fellow astrologer Reverend Cindy Buning has done extensive research on this theory. Over the past twenty-one years she has tested this age-old theory on over ten thousand people, and the findings were phenomenal.

I have heard some people call this theory Chinese Numerology. Others have called it Life Time Numerology. This can be an important tool in finding out where you're at, as far as spiritual growth, how old of a soul you are and what lessons you need to learn, with an emphasis on relationships.

If you fail to learn your lessons in your number one lifetime, it is believed you will repeat the number-one cycle over and over until you get it right. You can't move onto the next lifetime until you've passed the previous one. Think of someone in a first lifetime similar to a preschooler or kindergartner. By the time someone reaches their ninth lifetime, they'll graduate college and never have to come back!

Let's learn the formula first :

Take your day of birth,

Add that to your birth month,

Then add the last two digits of the year of birth,

Example: April 1, 1970 = 4+1+70 =75.

Add the number down to a single digit 7+5 = 12,

Then (12) 1+2 = 3.

The 3 indicates a Third Lifetime.

The Nine Lifetimes

First Lifetime

These are the babies, the young souls. This is their first experience on the physical plane. They make a lot of common sense mistakes. To them, everything is new. They stick with what they know. They appear to be childlike, immature and sometimes selfish. Some don't believe there is a God, and even more don't believe in the hereafter.

They have not developed specific personality traits and learn as they go. The younger the soul, the more mistakes it makes. These folks make many. They have to work hard at everything; marriage, parenting, and making the right choices. Their biggest challenge is to reach further out into world. They must learn to take the initiative.

They also need to work harder at understanding the mechanics of relationships and being more open to spiritual wisdom. They must learn where they've come from and develop faith in God.

Second Lifetime

These folks are here to work on relationships but not just those of a romantic nature. They'll try everything once and are learning that they need other people to survive. They need to learn how relationships work, their significance and the importance of having family, friends, parents, and mates.

The people in their number two lifetimes have a strong faith in God because that's what they had to learn in their previous lifetime. Their real challenge is compromise, appreciating others and learning to love.

Third Lifetime

These people are cautious. They like tradition, format and structure. They usually enjoy financial fortune. These are the salt-of-the-earth type of people who grow up in a community and never leave.

They avoid risky ventures and don't want to try anything "new age." They believe in God but don't have an overwhelming faith. They tend to be good husbands and wives, very family-oriented, loyal mates and friends. Their challenge is to have more faith in themselves and reach beyond what is considered safe and secure.

Fourth Lifetime

People in their fourth lifetime are rather conventional towards family and mates. They are a cross between the threes and the fives. They were born with certain goals they strive to accomplish.

There is a tendency to be cautious like the Threes, but at least they will question and explore the mysteries of life. When it comes to love, they like to pick a mate, settle down and live happily ever after.

Most of the Fours have predestined mates. They are the souls that agree to come back to marry a specific someone from a previous lifetime. Their relationships are usually long-term. They are more likely to go into therapy to work out issues than other souls. They will miss out on some opportunities life has to offer because they don't take enough chances. However, there are times when they can be very unpredictable.

Fifth Lifetime

Born with a list of things they want to do on the physical plane, fives are excited to be here. They are big dreamers with big plans. They have good luck but not overwhelming wealth. Some Fives can be very creative and make money through their own inventions. They share a strong faith in the hereafter.

Fives don't have consistency in relationships. Many enjoy more than their share of love affairs. They like variety in love. Many never marry or have been known to go without a personal relationship for years. They are comfortable with the life they are pursuing but don't find it necessary to have a mate. They are here to have fun, to play and lead an exciting life.

Fives' challenge is not to hurt people with their selfishness. They have to work on ego issues. They don't intend to hurt anyone but sometimes they do.

Sixth Lifetime

Sixes are here to inherit the world, but they have to first understand the physical plane, not just the earth, but the body as well. They need to learn how the body serves us, how to take care of it and make the most of it.

Some are born with health challenges. Once they learn the environment is very important to their health, they can overcome any health issues. If they understand the universe and how it works, they can achieve great things and possibly become very wealthy. This is a very materialistic lifetime.

You have to have this lifetime once so you can realize it's

not worth having. You can repeat this lifetime several times, but when you pass on, you learn to leave material wealth here.

Sixes are very family oriented but have to choose between the material world and their families. Sixes endure lots of karmic retribution in relationships. If they've laid good karma, they have loving mates. If they've laid bad karma, then relationships are difficult.

Their challenge is to let go of their materialistic needs so they can provide a balance between their personal relationships and their work.

Seventh Lifetime

This is a challenging lifetime. It is a karmic lifetime. Some sevens are born to be totally dependent on society. This is a cruel fate. Of the research done, many people in nursing homes and institutions were in their seventh lifetimes. Sevens are dependent on others. If not, then others are usually heavily dependent on them.

Whatever bad karma they have laid in the previous six lifetimes, they pay for it in the seventh. Also, sevens are more likely to contemplate suicide than any other of the lifetimes.

The challenge is to "stick it out" in the lifetime, out to the complete end, and accept all karmic debts graciously.

Eighth Lifetime

Eights enjoy a good money lifetime. The idea is to create a comfortable lifestyle and a better reality. Eights make great changes in the world to alter the state of reality. Here you find your gurus and spiritual leaders. Financially blessed, many eights are detached when it comes to personal relationships. They want to help the entire world, to promote love and peace and make major changes on the earth plane. They go forth to spread the word of God and usually have the money behind them to afford such a lifestyle. Their challenge is to use that spiritual nature for the highest good and stay away from manipulation.

Ninth Lifetime

Nines are happy but outsiders tend to look at nines as having very sad lives. Nines are closely regulated by God. If you're in your Number Nine Lifetime, you have no malice, no hatred and stay out of trouble.

If you do anything deceitful, you'll get busted every time. God keeps these folks in line. If they lie, they'll get caught. If they steal, they'll go to jail. Since this is the last lifetime, they need to be ready to leave the earth without great sin. They never own a lot, don't seem to amount to much and are not lucky financially. God makes it this way so that it's easier for them to leave the physical plane. There is less to let go of.

Nines have physical ailments. They are often uncomfortable in the body. They seem to carry extra burdens. This also helps them let go in this lifetime and not look back.

Nines appear to have bad relationships because they draw the younger souls whom they are here to teach. Their challenge is to stay spiritual no matter how hard things seem.

CHAPTER TEN

Creating the Love You Want

Everyone has an ideal love. If you haven't found yours yet, there are some things you can do to help the process along. In a previous chapter, we talked about accepting yourself, finding your purpose in life, becoming spiritually healthy and drawing what you need from the universe. There are a few more ways to increase your spiritual awareness, find your soul mate and create more balance in your everyday life.

Astrological Influences

If you're ready to find true love or just enhance your current relationship, the time must be right for doing so. An in-depth interpretation of your astrological chart can point out opportunity times for love, romance and commitment. Your chart can also show you the most likely places and times to meet love interests as well as the type of people you are most compatible with. For some people, their astrology charts can point out, what is holding them back from finding a decent relationship, as well as negative patterns to be aware of in current commitments.

Positive Affirmations and Visualizations

I tell my clients if you want something, you must visualize it twenty times. By that time it is ingrained in your brain. If you can believe it, you will see it. Write down everything you wish for in a mate. Make a wish list and then affirm it each and every day. Make affirmations a part of your daily prayers. A good novena to St. Jude wouldn't hurt, either!

Novena to Saint Jude

St. Jude is known world over as the patron Saint of the hopeless. Millions of people including myself have found this nine-day novena really works miracles.

Say the prayer for nine consecutive days. On the ninth day, your prayer will be answered. When you receive your blessing, you must publicize the prayer. That is why you see this novena printed in the classified ad sections of newspapers all over the world.

I prayed for a nice home in 1990. On the ninth day of my novena, my real estate agent called and told me my offer was accepted on a little, red farmhouse!

The same year, I prayed for a new job. On the ninth day, I saw an ad in the newspaper for a position tailor-made for me. I went to the interview and was hired!

Sometimes the prayer takes longer. One time, it took nine months for a special intention of mine to materialize. The number nine is significant. Many clients ask me for copies of this novena, so I thought it was important to include it in this book.

Prayer To Saint Jude
(To be said in desperate cases)

St. Jude, Glorious Apostle, faithful servant and friend of Jesus, the name of the traitor has caused you to be forgotten by many but the true Church invokes you universally as the Patron of things despaired of; pray for me, who am so miserable; pray for me, that finally I may receive the consolations and the succor of Heaven in all my necessities, tribulations and sufferings, particularly (make your request here) and that I may bless God with the Elect throughout Eternity. Amen.

St. Jude, Apostle, martyr and relative of our Lord Jesus Christ, of Mary and of Joseph, intercede for us.

Meditation

Meditate on receiving gifts for your highest good. When we meditate, we reach a higher consciousness. See clearly what you want in a relationship. Accept that it is being manifested for you.

When you meditate, it is important that you are not distracted. I suggest finding a private place in your home away from televisions, radio and other electronic equipment. Turn the phone and the answering machine off. Sit in a comfortable position with your eyes closed and head tilted slightly back.

- Clear your mind and inhale deep breaths. Slowly exhale, while counting, ten, nine, eight, seven, on down. Do this several times, until you feel light and open.

- Relax all parts of your body, starting from your feet on up. Continue and be aware of your deep breathing patterns.

- As you clear your mind, visualize what it is you are hoping to attain. If you have no urgent problems to solve, ask your higher self for any messages. You can stay in this higher conscious state for hours. Most people meditate for 15 to 30 minutes at a time. The length of the meditation is not as important as just taking the time to do it.

CREATING THE LOVE YOU WANT

The first few times beginners meditate, it's usually harder to reach a higher state. But with practice, people have been known to find their sacred spot within a matter of minutes. Most people can easily learn these techniques.

A good example of how easy it is to "drift" to a another level, is experienced when we're driving on a long, familiar highway. You know you have 40 miles or so to go, and you know your route very well. Your mind wanders off and you're not really focusing on the road but thinking of different things. Before you know it, you're at your destination. Time seemed to fly by! If you can relate to this example, you can easily adapt yourself to meditation.

When our minds are clear and open, we can often receive help from our subconscious. By relaxing our mind and bodies, we can solve problems easier, be more creative and decrease our stress levels.

Crystals

To create a more balanced "you," crystal energies and healing powers are good tools to consider.

Gemstones and crystals are part of nature, God's abundant creation. Crystals hold healing energies. These energies draw or vibrate to different things. One of the nicest crystals you can find for love and opening the heart chakra is the rose quartz. It is a soft pink color and helps heal broken hearts. It

CREATING THE LOVE YOU WANT

helps promotes self-love too. Carry a pink stone in your pocket or wear a rose quartz necklace to draw love and energy from the universe. Clear quartz crystal draws energy to you, as well. Amethyst helps spur on spiritual consciousness. Wear all three together to draw higher spiritual love!

When you choose a stone or crystal, I suggest you follow your intuition. If a crystal warms up in your hand, its energy will work for you. If it remains cool or cold to your touch, it's likely the energies of that particular stone are not responding to you.

For years I have had a strong desire to find pink tourmaline jewelry. Not pink ice or garnet. Even the beautiful pink sapphires would not do. I was drawn to the pink tourmaline. It is not the easiest gemstone to find. So whenever I ran across a ring or necklace, I bought it. I felt something was missing if I didn't wear the stone or carry it with me. There are different colors of tourmaline, but the pink is a heart stone that strengthens wisdom and willpower. It enhances creativity, too. The energies the stone had to offer me was something I needed at that time in my life. I don't wear the tourmaline as much as I once did but often find myself reaching for it at least once a week.

If there is something lacking in your life or perhaps some talent or virtue you'd like to strengthen, select a stone that enhances them. You'll likely notice subtle differences just after a few days.

There is another personal story I would like to share

with you. About ten years ago, I was going through a difficult separation in my relationship. I brought a rose quartz, heart-shaped pendant and wore it everyday. I even slept with the necklace. Rose quartz, as mentioned earlier helps heal broken hearts and brings love. I wore that stone for nine months until my ex came back into my life and wanted to work things out. The evening of our first date came and went. We had agreed to get back together. The next morning I realized my rose quartz necklace was gone! It was nowhere to be found. I searched high and low for the thing. The clasp to the necklace was strong so I knew it didn't break off. I came to the conclusion, the crystal had served its purpose and vanished. Its mission was completed. It played a part in bringing love back into my life. Other people have told me of similar experiences they have had with their crystals vanishing in thin air.

Crystals can be used to create energy, to open up chakras, and to help with emotional balance. When you first buy a crystal, it is important that you cleanse it or make it yours. Since crystals absorb energy, you should release other people's energies that have touched it before you use it. I always place my crystals in salt water over night. Never let anyone wear your crystals unless you want to carry their energy or issues around with you!

CHAPTER ELEVEN

Crystal Guide

Agate—Strengthens the body and mind. Helps with acceptance issues. Holds strength and courage. Powerful healer. Helps overcome difficult attitudes and promotes "truth."

Alexandrite—Positive influence on nervous system. Promotes joy. Connects one with higher self and angels. Aids in the body's regeneration, both internal and external.

Amazonite—Soothes nervous system. Helps strengthens heart and physical body. Also good for creative expression and communication. Gives wearer clear vision of negative tendencies or harmful addictions, making them easier to release.

Amber—Clears and balances emotions. Heals, soothes and brings harmony to wearer. Connects the past, present and future spiritually.

Amethyst—Calms and soothes. Increases intuition. Great for meditation and channeling. Helps thwart overindulgence. Many spiritual and healing energies. Helps wearer to find the truth. Powerful blood cleanser and energy giver.

Aquamarine—Reduces nervousness and fluid retention. Excellent meditation stone. Balances the physical emotional and mental states. Helps dissolve fears or phobias. Inspires peace, calmness and love.

Aventurine—Releases anxiety and fears. Stabilizes emotions. Comforts and supports. Brings a positive attitude to daily life. Strengthens blood.

Azurite—Enhances psychic abilities, helps healing facilities. Brings higher consciousness to wearer. Cuts through illusions. Good for meditation.

Bloodstone—Strengthens bloodstream, heart, spleen and bone marrow. Physical cleanser. Adds self-confidence and reduces emotional stress. Brings harmony. Gives inner guidance.

Barite—Has a harmonious influence on relationships.

Blue Lace Agate—Soothes emotions and pain. Relaxes and strengthens senses.

Calcite (clear)—Alleviates fear, balances male/female polarities. Gives clear perception of truth.

Calcite (green)—Releases fear and helps wearer to form new ideas to enhance life's power and goals.

Calcite (pink)—Releases old fears and grief. Helps provide unconditional love.

Calcite (amber)—Soothes inner disturbances. Guides changes and transitions, especially to a higher spiritual lifestyle.

Calcite (orange)—Gives sexual energies, clears negativity and aids in regeneration.

Carnelian—Gives personal power to wearer. Helps ground and focus thoughts. Used for infertility and impotence problems. Opens the heart. Aids lung, liver, kidneys and gallbladder.

Celestite—Reduces stress. Helps with thyroid problems. Promotes growth and creative personal expression. Gives clear speech.

Chrysocolla—Balances emotions. Reduces fear and anger. Helps upset stomach and arthritis. Helps speed up metabolism. Great for female disorders and helps clear subconscious imbalances.

Chrysoprase—Eases depression and sexual problems. Helps with fertility. Helps one see clearly and define personal problems. Brings out inner talents.

Citrine—Controls emotions and brings awareness and clarity. Enhances prosperity and body's natural healing energies. Raises self-esteem. Good for kidneys, colon, liver and heart.

Diamond—Breaks through blockages in the personality. Good healing stone. Increases will and power. Intensifies the power of other stones.

Dioptase—Good for ulcers, nervous stomach, heart trouble, blood pressure. Offers emotional stability and peace of mind. Great for using with affirmations and healing.

Emerald—Works on all matters of the heart. Draws love and kindness. Heart healer. Helps immune system. Enhances dreams, meditations and intuition. Brings prosperity, love and patience to wearer.

Fluorite——Good for meditation. Strengthens teeth and bones. Grounds excess energies. Helps wearer to focus. Powerful healing stone.

Garnet—Inspires passion and love. Sleeping with it helps you remember your dreams. Enhances imagination and brings compassion to wearer.

Gem Silica—This is a rare and beautiful stone. Helps discover feminine side. Helps men get in touch with their feelings. Used by women for female disorders, pregnancy and birth. Brings peaceful energies.

Hematite—Helps with grounding. Aids intuition. Reduces stress and helps circulate oxygen to the bloodstream. Enhances personal magnetism, will power and courage.

Jade—Promotes universal love. Radiates divine, unconditional love. Dispels negativity. Strengthens heart, kidneys and immune system. Increases longevity and fertility. Aids in dream study.

Jasper—Powerful healer on physical body. Good for bladder, gallbladder and liver.

Kansas Pop Rock—A mood enhancer. Attunes wearer to nature. Heals holes in auras. Give physical energy and happiness.

Kunzite—Good for people with addictive behaviors. Very high spiritual love vibration. Heals heartbreak. Enhances self-esteem and acceptance. Soothes, calms.

Kyanite—Gives creative expression and communication. Helps with astral travel. Promotes truth, loyalty and reliability.

Lapis—Increases intuition, spiritual growth and growth of personal relationships. A stone of royalty. Brings old, hidden emotional wounds to surface for healing.

Lepidolite—Strengthens muscles and heart. Aids sleep. Brings joy and light.

Lodestone—Magnetic rock. Realigns chakras and auric fields.

Malachite—Reveals subconscious fear and blocks. Great balancing stone. Good for pancreas and spleen. Reduces tensions.

Moldavite—Aids alignment with higher self. Aids in channeling. Balances physical mind and body.

Moonstone—Brings harmony to marriage. Relieves frustrations and balances emotions. Aids in psychic abilities. Lifts spirits. Aids birthing process and helps with female problems.

Obsidian—Connects mind and emotions. Has masculine energy. Removes negativity from the wearer. Teaches us how to find the true light. Dispels erratic behavior.

Onyx—Relieves stress. Aids wearer in detachment and self-control. Stops fear of the unknown. Helps control passion and negativity.

Opal—Absorbs energies and works with karma. Aids eyesight. Enhances intuition.

Pearl—Soften pains. Soothing, peaceful vibrations.

Peridot—Purifies body. Increases intuitiveness. Stimulates mind, but reduces stress. Helps accelerate personal growth.

Pyrite—Gives a more positive outlook on life. Helps one's ability to work with others in harmony. Enhances brain functions. Improves circulation and digestion system.

Quartz—The "everything" crystal. Magnifies the intensity of other crystals. Absorbs negativity in the wearer's energy field. Good for meditation and communication with spirit guides. Activates all levels of consciousness. Provides positive energy.

Rose Quartz—The love stone. Vibrates and draws love to those in need. Calms the heart and emotions tied to it. Clears stored anger, guilt, jealousy. Develops self-confidence and courage. Reduces relationship stress.

Rhodochrosite—Helps with matters of the heart and emotions. Unites the conscious and subconscious minds. Clears away old pains and hurts. Helps ease trauma. Blends divine love, acceptance of self and life.

Rhodonite—Promotes feelings of self-worth. Improves memory. Dispels anxiety and confusion. Draws love. Aids central nervous system and body reflexes.

Ruby—Provides wearer with a stronger heart and aids in the ability to love. Promotes zest and passion for life. Strengthens immune system.

Rutilated Quartz—Helps restructure cells. Energizes. Eases depression. Transmutes negativity.

Sapphire (Blue)—Helps with organizational skills and self-discipline. Gives psychic ability, creativity, loyalty and love. Helps with flow of spiritual energy.

Sapphire (Yellow)—Helps build creativity. Gives wearer strength and discipline to manifest creative ideas and projects.

Selenite—Strengthens teeth and bones. Gives clarity and concentration. Expands willpower.

Smoky Quartz—Good for depression and fatigue. Enhances dream interpretation and channeling abilities. Increases fertility. Good for sexual balancing.

Sodalite—Good for thyroid and pancreas. Calms as it helps clear the mind of tensions and stress. Good for enhancing communication and creative abilities. Works on relieving subconscious guilt and fear.

Sugilite—Often used by cancer patients. Strong protective qualities. Brings spiritual awareness. Reduces stress and helps with meditation and channeling.

Tiger-eye—Softens stubbornness. Gives clarity and spiritual perception. Helps one to see "both side of the coin".

Topaz (Blue)—Enhances metabolism, promotes tranquility, peace. Soothing effect on wearer. Gives creativity and self expression.

Tourmaline (Green)—Brings wisdom. Nurturing. Dispels fears. Aids sleep. Good for physical healing power.

Tourmaline (Pink)—Heart /love stone . Strengthens wisdom and willpower. Enhances creativity.

Tourmaline (Watermelon)—The best heart chakra healer. Releases old emotional wounds. Replaces pain with love.

Tourmaline (Black)—Offers protection from negative or heavy energies.

Turquoise—Tones entire body. Aids lungs, circulatory system. Gives peace of mind, friendship, loyalty. Very spiritual stone.

Variscite—Balances body and mind. Helps with past life recall. Brings abundance and prosperity. Aids heart, blood and emotional stability.

Zircon—All around healer. Strengthens the mind, self-esteem. Aids in sleep.

CHAPTER TWELVE

Maria Shaw's Numerology for Lovers

've designed my own Lovers Numerology formula to help you predict the next nine years of your love life. It is important to find your love year as well as your mate's. If you're single, this formula gives you insight on your most likely years for romance and marriage. If attached, the information can help you improve your current relationship and warn of coming challenges or crisis. The formula is simple to learn. You'll be amazed at how accurate it is. I've used this method for thousands of clients over the past ten years and it has never failed.

In this numerology formula, our lives run in nine-year cycles. Each cycle has a different meaning. We deal with different issues, and emphasis is placed on a certain point or path in our life each year. The cycles run from birthday to birthday rather than calendar year to calendar year. This is important to remember. I will explain the different cycles shortly.

*For, now, here's the formula you'll need to
discover your Love Number:*

First Step: Take your birth month and add it to your day of birth. (Do NOT include the year)

Example June 4th $\qquad$ $6 + 4 = \underline{\textbf{10}}$

This is the tricky part: You add the above number to the Current Year Master Number.

Current Year Master Number

1999 - 1

2000 - 2

2001 - 3

2002 - 4

2003 - 5 $\qquad$ 10

2004 - 6 $\qquad$ $\underline{+\ 2}$ $\quad$ (current year master number)

2005 - 7 $\qquad$ $= 12$

2008 - 8

2009 - 9

2010 - 1

The numbers repeat themselves every ten years.

Take that last number and deviate it down to a single digit. You always want to take the number down to its lowest single digit.

$$12 = 1 + 2 = 3$$

*Then you have your Love Number for the year.
In the example, it's the number three.*

It is extremely important to remember the Lovers Numerology does not run calendar year to calendar year. It runs from your birthday to your next birthday.

For example, if your next birthday falls on December 31, 2000, you cannot use the Master Number for 2000 until you reach your birthday. You will still be working off 1999's Master Number until the end of 2000. If your birthday is April 1, 2000, you will be working off the 1999 Master Number for the first four months of the calendar year. In April, begin using the 2000 Master Number.

Cycles of Love

Number One Year—This is a year of bright, beautiful beginnings. The emphasis is on YOU! Your needs, wishes and dreams will be the focus. I always tell my clients when you are in your Number One Year, you can get ANYTHING you want, but you need to ask for it. No one is going to hand you anything on a silver platter.

You can get anything if you go after it. You may have to ask more than once for your heart's desire, but it's likely that you will receive it. Anyone coming into a Number One Year should take the time to make up a wish list. This is most effective when done on your actual birthday. The list should include everything you want, big and small. It doesn't matter if some of the things sound silly. Just write them down. This is YOUR year. I recall a friend of my mine who put marriage at the top of her list on her June birthday. By October, she was married.

This is a great year to initiate NEW love. If you want a relationship, ask someone out. It's okay to be a little pushy in your Number One Year. If attached, this is a fine time to ask your partner for the things you need in the relationship. People in this cycle tend to be a little more self-centered. They are more into the "me" than the "we." But if a relationship is on the top of your list, make the most of this energy to draw your perfect love!

Number Two Year—The Two cycle is one of the bigger relationship years. It's not necessarily a romantic time. It's more apt to be time of reflection on individual needs in a relationship. If single, people are ready to begin dating. They have finally decided what it is they want and need in love. They will not settle for anything less in their Number Two Year. It's extremely important to these folks to find a partner at this time. They feel frustrated and lonely if single and usually put their best foot forward to meet new people.

For those people in a committed relationship, this is a year they appreciate their partner. They are happy just to be together. Any problems or issues that come up are easily addressed now. Love seems to be flowing through the Number Two Year person. They are very aware of what their needs are and not afraid to ask their partners to meet them. This is truly a "growing" period for a committed couple. Their relationship can reach new heights. One problem could arise, however. The partner who is experiencing the Number Two Year energy may feel so "in love" that they annoyingly smother the object of their affections.

Number Three Year—Communication, travel and creative pursuits fill this cycle. This is not an intimate type of year. This year holds appeal for doing things with friends and large groups. You will want to enjoy life. You won't care to deal with anything heavy. This is an excellent year for the unattached to get out and socialize. Single clubs, dating services and travel can bring new love interests into your life. Your friends will set you up on blind dates, too. Any clubs or organizations you join, could lead you to finding a romantic partner.

If you're in a relationship, the Number Three Year offers you and your partner a year to travel in together, to cast worries aside and just have fun! If you have trips you've placed on a back burner, now is the time to take them! Communication is strong between you and your lover during this time. This is not a commitment year although the subject could be discussed. It's more about enjoying one another's company, exploring new interests and letting the good times roll! Have all the fun you can handle now because when you hit your Number Four Year, there won't be time.

Number Four Year—This is the best year to advance in a career or business. It is not necessarily the biggest money year, but you can increase your income. If you do, it will be through your hard work.

This is a year in which love takes a back seat. Often your love life will be dull or you'll be too busy working to notice. You won't have time to get out and celebrate new relationships. If single, you could meet potential lovers through the work environment, but more likely, you will be too focused on climbing the career ladder to pursue anything else. If married, you will put all of your energy into your job. This may cause your mate to feel neglected.

You'll be successful in the workplace but be careful to balance work with your personal life so problems don't arise. You can create major changes in your career this year, expansion, promotions, new directions and the fulfillment of your highest goals. But even the strongest relationships could suffer if the home fires aren't kept burning.

Number Five Year—This is the year for the new love affair. This is also a year when you will have many romantic options. It seems as if everyone is interested in you. Don't turn anyone down for a date that has potential, at this time. Know that you will attract some wonderful people but you'll attract your share of losers, too!

The more you get out of the house, the better your chances become of finding the "Right One". I can guarantee that you won't be attracted to everyone who shows interest, but there will likely be at least one person you will want a relationship with before this cycle ends. This is not a marriage year. It is a year for romance and exploration. Do not limit yourself to just one person unless you feel you've met your soul mate. If a relationship doesn't work out, be patient: Someone else will come along. This is a year in which you can meet your marriage partner.

If married, and trying to start a family, the Number Five Year is the best year in which to conceive. It is also a time to watch out for little health concerns and take care of any right away.

This year your sex drive goes sky high! You feel more sensual and romantic. It is also a time that's ripe for an extra martial affair. The Number Five Year brings in attraction, when married or single.

I tell my single love-seeking clients this is the year they've been waiting for. Make the most of it. You will need to get out of the house. It's likely your dream lover is not the pizza delivery person.

Number Six Year—You will try to perfect your world during this period. The Number Six Year is the cycle in which you feel a strong desire to get your life in order. If you're not happy with your residence, you'll move. If you hate your job, you'll send out resumes.

This is a good time to break bad habits. You will have the

willpower to stick to a weight-loss or stop-smoking plan. Determination is this year's buzz word. The Six Year is a time when you get rid of what's not working for you and replace it with something that will. If your relationship is going nowhere and is way past its prime, you break it off with less guilt. It's easier to say goodbye now than three years from now, when you'll be in your Number Nine Year.

Likewise, if there are obstacles in a good relationship, you will work hard with your mate to overcome them. Singles could meet through relocation, group therapy and exercise groups. You may find a fabulous knockout at the gym while you're working at getting in shape yourself. You're feeling better about yourself and striving for a balance between your emotional, physical and spiritual well being. When you feel good, you look good. Others are naturally drawn to you.

Number Seven Year—This is a legal year. That also mean divorce or marriage aspects are favored. You could decide the lover you met in your Number Five Year is the one you'll walk down the aisle with now. This can be a very spiritual year. If the universe is going to reward you in love, you'll benefit this year. If you've laid bad karma, there could be breakups.

If a divorce in the Seven Year comes up, there's probably been handwriting on the wall. You may decide the marriage wasn't working or you've outgrown it while experiencing the effects of the Six Year. You will be luckier in legal matters this year and expect these types of issues to surface: loans, applications, real estate matters or lawsuits. Because the number seven is a very spiritual number, its year will be filled with higher thinking on your part. You could become enlightened about a spiritual path or the direction it takes for you and your partner. People you meet will likely have a profound effect on your life at this time. You will look at love and all of your relationships from a higher perspective.

Number Eight Year—This is an excellent money year. The Eight Year brings money to you effortlessly. Financial rewards do not always have to come via your work during this period. Gambling and investments may pay off quite handsomely. It is a possibility you could meet someone very wealthy or affluent who will shower you with gifts or opportunities.

Since you will have more money at your disposal, you can invest in hobbies and other interests. As you expand your horizons, you expand your social circle. If you are married, your partner could see a raise at work. Good deals and bargains are easily found. This is also a good year to reap the rewards of all of the hard work you've been putting into a relationship the past few years. Your partner will not only be more generous with money but with attention and affection, too. Since money is the number one reason couples fight, there shouldn't be much arguing during the Eight Year Cycle—except on how to spend the new cash flow.

Number Nine Year—This year wraps up your entire nine-year cycle. Here, we deal with the karma of the past eight years. Anything you didn't do or handle correctly in the previous cycles, you must address now. You have no choice. You will have to deal with the past, like it or not. Some people fear the approaching Nine Year. Others are not affected by crisis because they have lived the other cycles correctly.

Many times the past will come back to haunt you. For instance, if you didn't deal with a health issue in your Number Five Year, it could grow worse by the time you hit Number Nine. If you were supposed to get married two years earlier and called the wedding off, you could marry during this cycle. (Not necessarily the same person.) Also this is the year, ex-lovers come back to town. If you still have unresolved issues with a past amour, fate will bring you a chance to finish them. Your Number Nine Year doesn't always bring bad luck, but most of us don't always follow the straight and narrow. There are usually some things we must contend with. The least you will experience is a feeling of being "held back." It's as if you can't get ahead, no matter how hard you push. The universe is telling you to slow down. Allow yourself time to reflect. You'll be up and running when the Number One Year hits on your next birthday.

CHAPTER THIRTEEN

Compatibility Among The Sun Signs

I credit much of my success in my astrology practice to the fact that I specialize in relationships and affairs of the heart. Most people, when consulting an astrologer, want to know about love, career and finances, in that order.

I believe that most people can make any relationship work if they are aware of what makes their partner tick. If one can understand even the basic sun sign knowledge and characteristics of each sign, they have more ammunition when it comes to battle it out or call a truce.

Of course, there are sun sign combinations that work better than others. If you're a water sign, things will naturally flow easier with a Pisces, Cancer or Scorpio. Earth signs are compatible with you, too (Capricorn, Taurus, Virgo). Air signs (Gemini, Libra, Aquarius) mix well with fire signs (Leo,

Sagittarius, Aries) There are always exceptions to the rule but for the most part, it's safer to say you'll have an easier time with a compatible astrological partner.

You should also take into consideration a person's entire astrological chart. This would include the rising and moon sign, Venus and Mars. For the sake of keeping things simple for all readers, it will be sufficient to read your sun sign and your rising sign if you know it. Your rising sign is very important and can be obtained by getting a natal chart done by a professional astrologer. These days, you can likely find the information on the Internet.

If you aware of your love interest's birth date, you can make a better decision whether to further a relationship or not. If you're currently in a commitment, this chapter can help you understand the weaknesses and strengths of the relationship.

ARIES—The Ram

March 21–April 21

The ram has the most pioneering spirit of all the sun signs. Being the first sign of the zodiac, Aries enjoys and EXPECTS to be number one in personal relationships. If you've got your eye on an Aries, it is most important to remember to keep the chase going. Both men and women of this origin love the chase. The harder you are to catch, the more you'll find them clamoring for your affections. However, once the relationship gets too comfortable and too predictable, Aries lose interest fast. Aries loves being the center of their mate's world. They demand it! So your best bet is to love them for their strengths; directness, optimism, their need to succeed. It takes a strong, self-assured partner not to live in their shadows. If you need emotional attention and constant companionship, look to another sign, but I can guarantee that you will not be bored. Life and love with an Aries is nothing short of an adventure!

Aries are also the biggest flirts among the zodiac signs. They can easily date more than one person at the same time and frequently find themselves in "one niters." But when they fall in love, they usually fall hard and fast. They can spot those people who play mind games, for they play too! But what they really want in a long-term commitment is a strong partner. Remember they enjoy a challenge. Their biggest challenge however is to compete less and cooperate more.

Aries with Aries—This could be a decent match if you learn to let each other take turns leading. The biggest problems arise when both partners want to be the boss. These two hot heads will create the quarrels of the century but also can release that energy into an intense, passionate and fiery commitment. They will respect and admire each other, but their competitive nature will backfire in the relationship as time goes on. It is important that a marriage such as this does not fall into a rut. If both partners consistently bring their own ideals, ideas and individuality to the partnership, it has great potential. Aries women tend to be direct and to the point. Ladies, I must warn you that whatever you do, DO NOT bruise the Aries man's ego when it comes to the bedroom. He will get over an inferiority complex in the boardroom, but any jabs at his masculinity, will surely put the most arrogant Aries man's fire out.

Aries with Taurus—This could be a good sexual relationship and at times financially rewarding (especially for the Aries). But a long-term commitment, could spell disaster. Taurus are slow. They think things through. They save money. They enjoy the comforts of home and basically do not favor change. Aries are always throwing caution to the wind, spending their money spontaneously. They thrive on change. Many times, Aries think before they act. Taurus' need for emotional and financial security may not always agree with Aries' pioneering and independent attitude. Taurus can be extremely stubborn and cannot be pushed. Aries will learn patience from the Bull but will eventually refuse to live with it.

Aries with Gemini—Here are two quick-witted signs that love to talk. The Aries loves to talk about himself. Gemini loves to talk about everything and anything. Aries and Gemini will explore similar interests; travel, movies, higher intellectual pursuits. Even arguing can be fun between these two. Love can grow here. This is one of the better combinations. Both Aries and Gemini embrace change. They can't stand to be bored. These are the couples that plan skydiving for their first date, white water rafting on their second and a Las Vegas honeymoon on their third! So move out of their way and watch what happens. More times than not, their relationship will blossom quickly, grow, and endure.

Aries with Cancer—The initial sexual attraction between the Ram and the Crab is like a magnet! But watch out. We're mixing fire and water here. After the first few weeks, the whirlwind romance loses its momentum and it's all down hill from here. Cancer wants home and family; a mate who is on time for dinner, there when they need a shoulder to cry on and, most importantly, to nest with. But Aries has friends expecting them, places to go, people to see. Cancer feels rejected, hurt and abandoned. Aries cannot fathom Cancer's deep emotional and security needs. This relationship is going to require work, and I do mean hard work if it's going to last. On the up side, Cancer can provide a strong home base for the Aries when they must deal with any harsh realities of the world. Aries can show the moon children the lighter side of life, when they get a little too crabby!

Aries with Leo—These two signs are born leaders. Both aggressive, these signs complement one another. There could be a bit of competition, but it will likely prove to be invigorating. Romance and love will be highlighted: There will be satin sheets and scented candles mixed with sexual spontaneity. They will need to curb their spending enthusiasm and extravagance, but this couple will enjoy life and push it to the limit. Careers and social status will be very important in the union as well as friends, parties and hobbies. If Aries and Leo can put their own egos aside and work from their soul levels, this could be a dynamite combination.

Aries with Virgo—Aries are too headstrong and impatient to listen to Virgos nitpick, analyze and criticize. Virgos want everything perfect and will do all they can to "help" Aries become just that. The problem lies within the fact the Aries already thinks, excuse me, "knows," they are perfect. Thus, the Aries will look at the Virgo's helpful suggestions as nagging. The initial stage of romance seems grand, but as time drags on, the relationship wears thin. These two are not on the same wavelength. Aries could use their sense of humor to keep things going for a while. But the same old issues keep coming back. Virgo needs to be needed. After all, they are here to serve, but Aries ideas of servitude could be one-sided, leaving the Virgo feeling unappreciated.

Aries with Libra—They say opposites attract, and this certainly holds true for this fire/air combination. The Aries likes to lead and the Libra will allow it. This pairing usually works well and is considered to have long-lasting qualities. Both of these signs know how to flirt, Aries in an aggressive Martian way and Libra in a subtle Venusian style. Libra enjoy peace and harmony so they usually give in to an argument for the sake of keeping things tranquil. Aries learns they can keep pushing. For the most part, this couple can make it. Remember, Aries, do not take your partner for granted. And Libra, it's okay to speak up now and then. The Aries will respect and admire you all the more for it.

Aries with Scorpio—There is no way Scorpio is going to allow Aries to flirt outrageously and carry on in their usual manner unless, of course, it's between their own sheets. Aries will be deeply attracted to Scorpio's mysterious and sensual personality. Aries will enjoy the chase immensely but have regrets after the capture. They will find nothing gets past the Scorpio. There will be many emotional blowups, power battles and so on. A Scorpio will force the Aries native to dig deep and examine their emotional side, and that could scare the Ram. The way Aries and Scorpio look at life is different, too, especially concerning sex. I would suggest a working or business relationship, but love is going to feel like a wild roller coaster ride, with Scorpio in charge of the on/off switch.

Aries with Sagittarius—This can work. The Aries/Sag combo works because both parties are usually quite optimistic about life. This is the case where friends can become lovers. The two click in body and mind. They can sit and talk for hours. There is much satisfaction and encouragement between the Ram and the Archer. The downside is they could get in over their heads with their big ideas. Watch out for bankruptcy court rather than divorce court! This couple could enjoy travel to foreign lands. They'll encourage one another to achieve educational and career goals. They both like to seize the moment. If the love affair grows dull, they know when to part and can still remain friends long after the fire has gone out.

Aries with Capricorn—Capricorns play by the rules. They want a traditional, sometimes old-fashioned lifestyle. Aries are into trying anything new. Breaking rules is part of their pioneering spirit. So we have the past battling with the future. If these two could ever meet in the middle, a relationship just may work. But Capricorn is the sign of the Goat. They won't budge easily. These folks have strong, deeply imbedded opinions. Aries wants and needs to lead. First sexual attractions are strong but long-term probability is weak. This combination is good for career, but caution is advised for anything more than just a lustful look.

Aries with Aquarius—These lovers have just plain fun together—in work or play. Together, they could work on teaching and sharing their talents with the universe. They motivate one another. In a love affair, this combination works in harmony as long as Aries truly sees the Water Bearer's vision and allows them the freedom to pursue their dreams. Aquarius will help Aries expand their intellectual curiosities about the New Age. I do not see this duo as romantic, but passionate about their commitment. True friendships have been formed between Aries and Aquarius, and I have seen many marriages succeed with this combination of fire and air.

Aries with Pisces—The water sign of Pisces could easily put the fire sign of Aries out. Aries gets all excited about a new project, and Pisces immediately dampens the enthusiasm by pointing out the pitfalls. There is one connection between these two, and I'm not so sure it's a healthy one. Pisces tend to make personal sacrifices for their mates. They put them on a pedestal. Sometimes they take on all of their partner's problems. Aries, as we know, love to sit at the top of pedestals. They don't mind one bit if they are on the receiving end of a relationship. This could easily become a one-sided love affair as long as Pisces plays their martyr role so well. Aries could lose interest after a while and go looking elsewhere. I suggest a "just friends" approach from the get-go.

Taurus—The Bull

April 21–May 21

I always say earthy Taurus folks need only three things to make them happy: money, sex and food. Not necessarily in that order. But if your needs run along the same gamete, add security, fidelity and a nice home, you've probably met a soul mate.

Taurus has the reputation of being stubborn and, let me assure you, this is not an exaggeration. Coming from someone who knows firsthand, yes, Taurus men are stubborn, unyielding, at times can be lazy and grump a lot. But they are also steadfast, dependable and loyal.

Taurus of both sexes want long-term commitment. They don't like change. That's why so many born under this sign stay in relationships that are going nowhere. Once they have a goal in mind, Taurus stick to it. So if you have the caught the attention of one of these Bulls, watch out! They may take their time getting around to asking you out, but don't think for a minute they're losing interest. That's just Taurus's route to love. They sit back, think about asking you out, reflect some more, relax a little, think about you again and then, maybe you'll get a phone call.

When you do get around to a date, expect a refined, reserved date, possible a little too conservative. When you get around to a full-blown commitment, expect a sensual, exciting, but possessive and jealous partner.

Most Taurus want the best life has to offer. They enjoy fine wine, food, music, art and luxury homes. They take quality over quantity. They are also good money managers. You will never go hungry if you marry a Taurus.

But you will learn what a "hot temper" really is. Taurus is slow to anger but when they let loose, watch out! They are like a bull in a china store! Run for cover. The Taurus women are just as ornery as the men.

For the most part, the Bull is not prone to infidelity and expects the same from a partner. But if you happen to stray, even once, pack and take your belongings with you. Otherwise you'll never see them again, and you bet that goes for the Taurus, too.

Taurus with Taurus—Taurus men are all man and Taurus women very feminine. These two have the same basic needs, which include financial and emotional security. This pairing usually works better than other same sign partners. But at times, these two can be like a couple of old war horses not budging on issues and clashing in major power struggles. Jealousies can easily arise but think of the money to be made! The biggest question of all is, who will hold the checkbook?

Taurus with Gemini—I have seen this partnership work effectively with my parents. They were married over 50 years. The steady, secure Bull helps ground the youthful Gemini. They offer stability so Gemini can play and seek out their goals in life. This is one combination in which money is easily produced, and working together seems to work. There are differences in how each perceives spending and saving. Love grows deeper over time. Crisis makes these couples more committed. It doesn't always work, but it has a better chance than other air/earth combinations.

Taurus with Cancer—This is usually a keeper. One of the best matches in all of the zodiac. Both are homebodies. Both need financial security. Both are loving, affectionate, committed people who marry for life. However, Taurus can be too unyielding and set in their ways for Cancers who enjoy bossing. Any type of criticism will send Cancer into tears and they will remember everything you said, the date, time and place of the offense and make sure to bring it up years later, if needed. Cancers must learn not to take things too personally and just remember the old Bull is never going to leave you. You're, stuck but you probably like it that way.

Taurus with Leo—Here's a combination you hear doesn't work. That's mostly true. But in my practice, I have surprisingly found that many of these Taurus/Leo marriages can last. I have noted that in all of these successful marriages, both parties worked long hours, ran their own businesses or we're so committed to climbing the career ladder, they had no energy left to argue about anything. In general, Leos can be a little too dramatic and flashy for the down-to-earth Taurus. Those that do take the time to fight know the Leo will not give up the crown. Both signs need to know they are truly loved and if the ego/power struggles in this relationship are too great, both parties will be left feeling empty.

Taurus with Virgo—This is a nice combination; two earth signs that appreciate the value of a dollar. Virgos are known to be the best shoppers, and Taurus can trust their money is not being spent foolishly. Their needs are not extravagant and they enjoy each other's company. Taurus loves to be pampered and Virgo loves to be helpful and kind. So they are on the same page. There may be problems, however, when it comes to diet and health. Taurus loves to eat. It is one pleasure in life they will not be denied! Virgos are good cooks but they worry too much about their health and everybody else's. Taurus won't want to munch on carrots and other rabbit food for dinner. As long as Virgo remembers the way to a Taurus' heart is through their stomach, all will be fine.

Taurus with Libra—Both Taurus and Libra, are ruled by the planet Venus, so there will initially be a mutual understanding and attraction between these two signs. However, Venus works differently in each sign, and Libra's love of friends and spur of the moment parties will not go over well with Taurus' well-planned routine. The physical desire is there, but for long-term commitment, there could be problems with possessiveness on the Bull's part. Libra won't be tied down too long. They will bend only so far to keep the peace. The Taurus has a habit of becoming too condescending in relationships if things don't go their way. But this comes from insecurity rather than anything else. They are afraid of losing the Libra to their friends or other VIPs.

Taurus with Scorpio—Hot, Hot! Hot! Take the best sex sign in the zodiac, Scorpio, and place them with the stamina and sensuality of Taurus the Bull, and you can't get a better combination for erotica. But watch out, the fires don't just heat up in the bedroom. This could be an endearing long-lasting relationship or the most dangerous one these two will likely encounter in one lifetime. One thing is for sure: If they part ways, they both will look at love in a completely different way. This is the type of relationship that is either very good or very bad. There is no in-between. I think the longer the Scorpio and the Bull stay together, the more challenges they will meet successfully. In turn, their bond grows stronger and then nothing can break these two apart. The key is to forget about who has the upper hand, and just go for it.

Taurus with Sagittarius—I don't find this combination common. It is a good financial partnership. The Sag will help the Bull look at things from a different perspective. Perhaps teach them about new religions, philosophies, spirituality and maybe even about love. However Taurus the Bull could stomp on Sagittarius's freedom-loving ways. This will leave the Archer feeling suffocated and smothered. For a Sagittarius, a fate worse than death! I don't see how this relationship can experience longevity. The Sag will eventually break free if the Taurus doesn't change their possessive ways. But it's not within the Bull's nature and best interest, so leave this pairing for business and money making ventures only.

Taurus with Capricorn—These two earth creatures can see eye to eye on most things. I'm not so sure the sexual excitement will be as strong between these two as with other couples, but there is a deeper agreement when it comes to the way life should be lived. The two share a strong work ethic and will save money for old age. At times the relationship may seem dull but I don't foresee anyone leaving on that account. No, it would have to be a major faux pas: infidelity, abandonment or a hidden bank account the other partner knew nothing about.

Taurus and Aquarius—This is a crazy combination. There will be many ups and downs caused by a lack of understanding one another's personality type and basic needs. Taurus need to feel secure and to stay with the known. Aquarius need change. They crave it. It's almost as if they need change in order to survive. In the beginning of such a relationship, the Taurus may go along with trying new things the Aquarius introduces. It could be as simple as foreign food, travel or New Age ideas. But the longer the relationship goes on, the stronger the Bull will resist the new concepts. Aquarius will find themselves fighting to keep their true identity and wondering what went wrong. Sometimes this match works if the Taurus allows the Aquarius the variety and change they need. The Taurus may not always agree or understand the Aquarius' unusual ways, but in order for such a relationship to sustain, the Bull has to at least accept them if they can't embrace them.

Taurus with Pisces—Pisces can add a bit of magic to a Taurus' mundane world. They turn an ordinary day into a mystical journey. The practical Taurus seldom allow theirselves to get caught up in the fairy tale of life. Pisces will help Taurus experience the joy of escaping for a while, through meditation, art, music, perhaps, even daydreaming. Taurus will usually find this exhilarating but keep Pisces from going too far by bringing them back to reality. This earth/water combination can do well when they learn to take the best of both signs and blend the spiritual and practical sides together.

Taurus with Aries—After they get done deciding who's going to take the lead, these two could get much accomplished. For long-term love, however, there is much more needed to sustain this union. Taurus will not overreact, be pushed, convinced, bribed or shoved into anything they don't want to be. Aries just may be too impatient to wait for the old Bull to come around to his or her way of thinking. The fires could go out rather quickly for Aries waiting for the Taurus to light up. I would rethink this one.

Gemini—The Twins

May 21–June 21

Loving a Gemini is like having an affair. You're in love with two people. My clients always get a grin when I suggest this. Gemini is the sign of the Twin. There are two of them, you know. I usually go on to explain the good twin/evil twin theory. The twin you see the most of, is a good indicator of how your relationship is panning out with these beloved sun signs.

When happy, they talk and I do mean talk. Gemini will talk upon rising in the morning and while brushing their teeth. They talk to you while you're on the phone with someone else. They never shut up! As you're falling asleep, they are still talking. I guess you could say communication is important to Gemini in a relationship. So is mental stimulation. The Gemini needs it to enjoy a good love life, or they don't hang around too long. They are similar to small children, enjoying variety, change, losing interest in this and wanting that. That's the way it is with a Gemini in love. This is one sign that's better off to settle down in their forties rather than in their twenties or even thirties. Gemini is a youthful sign. They believe the universe will supply all of their needs. At the same time, Gemini can be the biggest worry warts. The twins are humanitarian too.

They are for the underdogs. Gemini bring home the lost puppies and cheer the losing team on. There is something about the Gemini you will find yourself drawn to. It must be their creative side. Or is it their intellect? Who knows? But the combination of the two personalities lends itself to an interesting relationship. Gemini can be fickle, however, in love, and anything dull, boring or restricting turns them off. They are unique people; people who can look at the world through the eyes of a grownup but with the heart of child. They have endearing qualities and often look years younger than they actually are.

The down side to this sign is that there are more con artists and liars born under this position. It must be that evil twin. If you think you're up to dealing with the personality and mood swings of a Gemini, you will certainly enjoy a relationship with this multi- faceted sign.

Gemini with Gemini—It's like living with four people! Putting two twins together may be too much. There will be plenty to talk about but if no one is doing the listening, there's bound to be problems. This could still work, although personally I feel the whole relationship could be a little overwhelming. I suggest taking turns, working as hard as you play at the relationship and keeping "the evil one" in check. It could be worse. You could end up with someone who doesn't communicate.

Gemini with Cancer—This is an excellent combination for casual dating relationships. But a walk down the aisle would need to be reconsidered. Cancer would likely take on the role of the parent to the young-at-heart Gemini, and joint bank accounts would not be a good idea unless Cancer was in charge of all finances. Cancers spout gray hairs early in life, married to Gemini. If kept light, the romantic, unattached couple would have long walks, wonderful talks, and shared interests.

Gemini with Leo—This team makes for interesting conversation. Compatibility is here for the most part. When brought together, both have the tendency to talk about home, family life, and early upbringing. There will be some issues to work on between the two, most notable Leo's desire to talk about himself all the time and Gemini's need to discuss more worldly matters. Family will be a great source of concern or contentment. If there are stepchildren involved, difficult in-laws and the like, it is important that the couple do not draw battlefield lines but work together as a team. When in the courting stages, if Leo is ready to whisper sweet nothings, Gemini needs to stop talking long enough so as not to miss the proposal. Good listening will be one of the key ingredients needed to make this union last.

Gemini with Virgo—In the beginning of such a relationship, there could be an immediate attraction but as time drags on, these two seem to constantly disagree about everything. These are very intelligent people for the most part, but put them together and you wouldn't believe the jabs. There is an irritating quality to their relationship. They don't like to be around one another for very long, but they can't stand being apart for any length of period, either. Stay clear unless you're absolutely sure it's true love.

Gemini with Libra—The pairing of these two air signs suggests a long-term commitment. There is something familiar and safe when Gemini and Libra come together. Gemini will find the Libra's intellect stimulating, as well as their physical attributes. They can be best buddies as well as marriage partners. These two could enjoy the same hobbies, music and sports. Children will play an important role in their lives if they chose to have a family. The major threat of separation could come during the mid-life crisis of one of the partners. Therefore, it is of utmost importance that ideals and expectations of the marriage are discussed, as often as needed, to avoid breakups.

Gemini with Scorpio—I'm not so sure Gemini could handle Scorpio's strong need for isolation. Scorpio personalities hold much of their thoughts and desires deep within. They communicate through sex. Gemini's constant need for mental stimulation finds no outlet here. Scorpio will be entertained by the Twins but not find the depth they are seeking in this particular sun sign. Jealousy and restrictions could lead to the downfall of this coupling. Great for friends and perhaps working buddies, but for serious, long-term love, save yourself time and heartache, Gemini.

Gemini with Sagittarius—Here is a case of opposites attract. For the most part, this could be a lively, healthy and prosperous pairing. Both signs love travel and change. Sag can talk about religions and philosophies and Gemini will find these chats interesting. They will show each other different viewpoints and an opposite way of looking at the world. However, both can be fickle in love. They'll flirt with everyone at a party. At least, they'll leave together. Life's bigger picture is emphasized here, and attraction is usually mutual. Even though both of these signs possess a wandering eye, the settled Gemini and Sag instinctively seem to know they're not going to stray too far from home.

Gemini with Capricorn—Simply stated, this is the young versus the old. Capricorn is the old sign of the zodiac. They live by the rules and relate well to tradition. Gemini is the child in this relationship, breaking all of the rules and a few hearts along the way. They can learn from one another. Capricorn can learn to get in touch with their inner child, to enjoy the silly in life, to take the time to reflect. Gemini can learn discipline, duty, responsibility and honor. But watch out, Capricorn, because the Gemini will likely break free and wreak havoc in your finely structured life, turning the elite world you've built for yourself upside down. I have seen many affairs between these two signs, due to the fact that each sign has what the other one lacks. But marriage will seem like an uphill battle. At the least, it will be a scenario of one step forward, three steps back.

Gemini with Aquarius—These two air signs are a solid combination. There could be many happy times. Each rolls with the flow and is ready to experience the changes and challenges that life has to offer. They will strive to make theirs the perfect love affair, different from any kind they've toyed with before. They can succeed. The Twins and Water Bearer know communication is very important and work to make sure each other's needs are fulfilled. Gemini will adore Aquarius' quirkiness and marvel at their sense of humor. Aquarius will strive to make sure Gemini is following their highest spiritual path.

Gemini with Pisces—If these two decide to marry, it is likely escapism will come into play at some point down the road. There will be a denial of truth to the marriage. Communications will be strained. Hurt feelings and misunderstandings will arise. The Pisces personality could drown their sorrows with food, drink or work. They eventually turn away emotionally. Gemini could live a separate life outside of marriage. There is often a feeling of never truly being married when these two signs join hands. In good Gemini/Pisces combinations, we usually see creativity play a major part in keeping the home fires burning.

Gemini with Aries—Gemini will love the way Aries entices them. They will enjoy the expansion of the mind and learning new things here. Aries plays the role of the teacher well and is more than happy to do so. It is important to note that both signs can be into mind games, so honesty and integrity should not be taken lightly in this particular relationship. There has to be physical attraction between these two, coupled with a sense of humor, to make this union long lasting. It's a safer bet than most, but caution needs to be exercised in expressing opinions differences. Otherwise, a simple question over what to have for dinner could lead to all-out war! The overall picture looks bright and promising. Much success is predicted when they work together on the meeting of the minds.

Gemini with Taurus—This is not the best combination for a successful relationship, but I have seen it work more times than not in my practice. I feel the key to these long-lasting unions must be the Taurus' patience with the Gemini, and the acceptance of what each sign needs. As long as Gemini is willing to play the games the Taurus wants to play, things will go well. But if Taurus can't get past Gemini's spending habits, unstructured lifestyle and constant need for variety and change, they will eventually break ties. The success of this commitment comes down to acceptance. It can be trying and difficult in the early years of marriage but has a long-lasting quality as times goes on.

Cancer—The Crab

June 22–July 22

These people are the "feelers" of the zodiac. They experience the highest joys and the lowest lows. Ruled by the ever-changing Moon, Cancer moods swing back and forth. They are the most sensitive and psychic sign of the zodiac. Because of their sixth sense, they make wonderful parents, therapists, teachers and doctors.

If a Cancer's childhood was secure, peaceful and encouraging, they grow up to be healthy, well-adjusted partners. If their childhood was filled with negativity, absent parents or shaky foundations, they could be messed up for life! Therapy is necessary to help these Cancers come out of their shell and face relationships without hesitation or the fear of rejection. Rejection is Cancer's worst fear. They value emotional security in love just as much as financial security.

They can be rather bossy and overprotective yet make excellent parents. Their children come first, with husband and dear old mom in a tie for second place. They are loyal, dependable, caring and kind.

Cancers enjoy travel, but home is where the heart is. They seldom move far away from their birthplace. Because of the Cancer's easy-going nature, many people are surprised as to just how determined a Cancerian can be. They never do anything they don't want to do. They can't be pushed.

During my many years of research, I have found Cancer is the sign that repeatedly sees the return of old flames and ex-lovers. It doesn't seem to matter if the relationship ended on a sour note ten or twenty years ago.

Most Cancers will meet up with their past. One of the problems Cancers have is that they, too, live in the past. They have remarkable memories. They will remind you of that horrible name you called them during a heated argument in 1970 and probably recall what clothes they were wearing too. They save all sentimental mementoes from dates and special occasions.

But because they live in the past, they feverishly won't let things go. Past love floods their imagination of "what could have been" and often ends up driving a wedge between them and their current partner. So it's important before getting involved with a moon child to make sure there are no skeletons hidden in their closet.

If you decide to further this affair, be warned: Cancer will accept nothing less than marriage and kids. No short-term, live-in arrangements for them! You will have the home you desire, the dinner on the table at five p.m. and a marriage full of feeling.

Cancer with Cancer—Home and family will be the focus, if these two decide to nest. There could be in-law problems. There is mutual understanding and the same security needs. Children will be a necessity in this marriage. One can lift and nurture the other's spirit through crisis. Cancer men make their women feel safe and protected. Cancer women baby and pamper their men. If trust is ever broken, though, through extra martial affairs, it is likely this union would not survive. Even if they agree to forgive, Cancers never forget.

Cancer with Leo—This relationship mixes fire and water. Though, it lacks in some areas, there can be a magnetic draw between the two signs. If Cancer can handle Leo's need to be the King or Queen of the Castle, things will go fine. If the throne is threatened, Leo can become overbearing and insulting, thus hurting Cancer's fragile feelings. The key is for the Crab to allow the Lion to "think" they are in charge, all the time calling their own shots behind the scenes. Leo's heart of gold will touch Cancer deeply but If children take up all of Cancer's attention and energy, the Leo will feel set aside and that just won't do! There are needs and ego issues that will have to be dealt with in this combo.

Cancer with Virgo—Water and earth signs work well together. Cancer will appreciate the little things the Virgo will do around the home. They both know how to squeeze a dollar out of a dime. Both are the best shoppers of all the zodiac signs. Bargains seem to drop into their laps. Cancers, however, will not appreciate Virgo's criticism, especially if it has to do with their mother, their cooking or their weight. Virgos like to help. They feel by suggesting improvements, they are helping their mates. Virgo should compliment their Crab and make them feel secure. In turn, Cancer will work hard to bring pleasure to the Virgo's everyday world.

Cancer with Libra—This is the homebody versus the socialite. Cancer will likely be left crying on the couch while Libra is out on the town in this match. Being with a Crab means you must give constant support, and Libra has all they can do to balance their own lives. There is much physical attraction in the beginning stages of this type of love, but eventually the same old routine takes over. The same scenes will be played out. Cool Libra will not understand Cancer's emotional mood swings. Libra will work at keeping peace and harmony, but Cancer will want to stir things up, to cry a little, perhaps pout. All they want is attention and to know they are loved! Libras will be looking for the closest exit sign. Better for friends than lovers.

Cancer with Scorpio—The intense emotional nature of these water signs blends easily. They may not consider one another moody or irrational as others have suggested they are. However, The Crab and the Scorpion are both master manipulators. They manipulate in different ways. If defeated, the Crab will back up, side step and then move in from a different angle to get their way. Scorpio usually wins by seducing or hypnotizing you with their eyes or sharp intellect. As long as these two are working on the same goals and there is strong trust, great things can manifest in such a relationship. Both are very psychic. But Scorpios need to show their feelings more when dealing with Cancers. They need to take communication farther than just the bedroom for Cancers to be completely satisfied.

Cancer with Sagittarius—Short-term, this duo is a great experience! Long-term commitments prove to be challenging, heartbreaking, and at the least, confusing. The fiery sign of Sag wants freedom. These are the Don Juans of the zodiac. The Sag woman is more patient than the Archer man, but that makes no difference when you pair them with a Crab. Sagittarius is trying to escape everything Cancer stands for: home, security, consistency. Sag may enjoy this treat for while, but then it's back to exploring what's out there in the world (and this means other relationships too). Cancer will never understand the need for Sag to roam. They just hate feeling smothered. They look at love and sex in much different ways. Sagittarius people are into truth. They tell it like it is. And that may be too much truth for the Cancer to bear. This match produces exciting short-term love affairs for there is immense attraction. But when the Cancer gets stars in their eyes, things will start going downhill fast!

Cancer with Capricorn—Sometimes this works. Much depends on how deep the emotional needs of the Cancer are. Capricorns are very stoic. They are logical and direct. Many cannot understand their own feelings much less their partners. Why concentrate on abstract things? If the Cappy is too cold and rigid, the Cancer will eventually look for emotional fulfillment elsewhere. What the Goat lacks in emotional ability, they make up for in the financial arena. This could prove to be a money making couple, especially in later years. Sexual attraction is very strong between these two. More than likely, the natives will miss one another desperately when they are apart and irritate each other when together. However, the relationship does have lasting potential.

Cancer with Aquarius—This is one, if not the worst, sign for Cancer to be associated with. Aquarius crave change more than any other sign. Their cool, aloof nature clashes with the homey, deep feelings Cancer possess. Many Aquarius do not find much use for the family they were born into. They can check in once or twice a year. The Cancer cannot cope with or understand Aquarius' detachment in relationships. Aquarius won't have time to make small talk about hurt feelings. They have a mission! They want to touch the entire world and make it a better place in which to live. In fact, their missions in life become more important then their partner. That's because Aquarius' spiritual path is helping humanity as a whole. But if they fail to keep the home fire burning with Cancer, it will eventually be put out.

Cancer with Pisces—If the man in this relationship combo is strong and secure, there will be much success and happiness. If weak, there will be problems with negativity, moodiness and possible escapism (alcohol or drugs). Usually the Crab and the Fish do just fine. They both are sensitive, psychic beings. Romance plays a big part in the initial courtship. There is mutual satisfaction, trust and the ability to communicate their feelings without fear of rejection. The research I have done also shows there are more millionaires born under the sign of Pisces than any other in the zodiac. There are more **self-made** millionaires, born under the sign of Cancer. So, this couple could see their dreams come true in a big way!

Cancer with Aries—The sexual attraction is strong between these two. This relationship allows the couple to experience love on the fast track. But it's a big gamble. Long-term relationships tend to fizzle out, leaving Cancer feeling rejected. While Cancer is still mulling over what went wrong, Aries is already out, flirting about town, ready for the next conquest. To Aries, the excitement in a relationship is the chase. For Cancer, it's the capture. They want to build foundations and securities. Aries could feel fenced in or bored. This relationship could work if the couple worked a family business together; otherwise, they are both living in their own worlds.

Cancer with Taurus—Cancer and Taurus fit together like a comfortable pair of jeans and a cozy old sweater. The relationship grows better with time. Cancer's security and financial needs get met. Taurus' hearty appetite is met in the dining room as well as the bedroom. This can be a long-lasting union, but their closets will be bursting. These two don't discard anything. Clothing, antiques, photos, newspapers—anything that has a purpose is salvaged and saved. That's the way the Crab and the Bull feel about their relationship, too. If it's worth saving, they'll stick together through the hard times and grow stronger because of it.

Cancer with Gemini—If they play together, they can stay together. But more often than not, Cancer assumes the role of the domineering, over protective parent of the Gemini. Then the relationship becomes one-sided. If these two can work on things as a team, there's smoother sailing. It's not your best bet, but Gemini will help the Cancer loosen up and teach them to play. Gemini will find Cancer someone to trust, to feel safe to be their "twin selves" with, and most all Cancers will listen. Talkative Gemini will appreciate the fact that someone is listening sincerely and maybe even taking notes. They will know they are being heard because Cancer's famous memory will point out declarations of love from years past and unfortunately recall the arguments too. For these two, love doesn't always last, but the friendship certainly can.

Leo—The Lion

July 23–Aug 24

Leos are said to have the biggest hearts among all the signs of the Zodiac. Proud, daring, sometimes arrogant, Leo will wear their hearts on their sleeves when in love. They often give 150% to their mates. Sometime they come on too strong but it's just because they find you the perfect showpiece for their regal arm.

In love, they are generous, but if left ignored or unappreciated, they are difficult beings to be around. Their need to be the center of their lover's universe is undeniable. The bigger the ego, the harder they fall. That's why Leos in love are so vulnerable. They give and give and give. They do expect some things in return: undying love, praise, loyalty and most of all respect. To disrespect a Leo, is the ultimate sin.

The way to capture a Leo's heart is to let them lead, to make them feel grand about themselves, and, of course, lay on those compliments. Be warned, Leo knows the difference between true admiration and hogwash. They enjoy being noticed and many take great care in the appearance of their hair (the lion's mane).

In marriage, the Leo needs to rule the roost with their loyal servants listening attentively to their ramblings and opinions. If their followers are indeed loyal, they will be blessed time and time again with Leo's generous spirit.

Leos are fun people. They like to live life large. Social status is very important to them. They want the best for the people they love and often work long hours to be able to give them the finer things in life.

Love keeps Leo alive. A Leo without love in their life is like an empty shell. Loveless Leos will try to fill the void with addictions such as gambling, shopping, drinking, or working too much.

Remember: If a Leo is happy, then everyone is happy. It's as simple as that.

Leo with Leo—This will be a dramatic relationship. The question to be answered is who will serve as the Royal Highness. Will they agree to share the spotlight or fight for it? There will be much love and admiration, and these two will make an engaging, attractive couple. It will be no problem choosing birthday gifts. Anything big, shiny or gold will do! Problems could arise if one partner is not supportive of the other's career goals. This union is sure to include temper tantrums but heavy doses of laughter and good times, too.

Leo with Virgo—Since Virgos like to be of service and need to be needed, the match up with the Majestic Leo sometimes works well. Leo rules. Virgo obeys. As long as this cycle remains intact, things will run smoothly. If Virgo rebels and tries to overpower the throne, there's likely to be a royal rumble. Note to Leo: Virgos who feel like servants don't serve as well as those who feel appreciated. Note to Virgo: Picky Virgos who criticize and make jokes at Leo's expense will find their services no longer needed.

Leo with Libra—There is potential with this pair. Libras are beautiful people and Leo likes a showpiece. Leo will also appreciate Libra's peacekeeping ways. Libra will allow Leo to lead and be happy to follow. There's one catch, though. Libra expects to be generously rewarded for what they have to offer. The finer things in life that Leo can so astutely provide are important. Plus, with Leo working day and night to keep the payments up, Libra has plenty of time to socialize and enjoy the little extras. Both signs are romantic and giving. They will enjoy shopping together and finding other creative ways to spend their money!

Leo with Scorpio—The handwriting is on the wall before this relationship gets off of the ground. Run! Run fast! Don't look back! But if you've already decided to try this combination out for yourself, expect major control issues. Keep a box of Kleenex nearby or better yet, a suit of armor. These fixed signs seldom find what they're looking for in one another. The sexual arena will be hot for a while, but Scorpio will not allow anyone to truly conquer them. The Leo will deal with their frustrations ferociously for a while and then probably just give up.

Leo with Sagittarius—Of the three fire signs (Aries, Leo and Sagittarius) the Archer works better with Leo. Sag draws energy from the two other fire signs. While Aries rules the head and Leo rules the heart, Sagittarius combines the head and the heart. You won't find the power struggles between Sag and Leo like you will between the Lion and the Ram. Sagittarius will contribute to Leo's positive and enthusiastic outlook on life rather than compete with it. The two will love to travel to foreign places, enjoy lively conversation and can settle comfortably into a long-term commitment. Part of this is so, because Sag doesn't take Leo's commands too seriously. These two can expand each other's world in many favorable ways.

Leo with Capricorn—Capricorn does not have a place in their structured, traditional lifestyle for flashy, overbearing egos. That is how the Goat may view the Lion at first glance. Usually first dates between these two signs go nowhere and often end early. If a second date is even considered, Capricorn may catch a glimpse of Leo's good work ethics and hard-driven spirit. I still conclude that these two would make better business partners than anything else. They both agree that career and social status are important. They just don't agree on much else. Coming from two different perspectives, they could learn much from spending time in one another's world but the initial attraction would likely fade.

Leo with Aquarius—While Leo is all about "Me," Aquarius is about "We" as in "We are the World." Aquarius could get Leo to stretch a little beyond the norm and that support will make the Lion grateful. Working together toward a common bond will keep Aquarius happy. Social clubs, fund-raisers, mutual friends are all important to keep this relationship ticking. If Leo curbs the tendency to roar out orders, Aquarius will stick around. Both sides enjoy experiencing new things, and this relationship will work well as long as the couple is open to moving, updating education, self-improvement and keeping up with the times.

Leo with Pisces—Most water/fire sign combinations don't work too well. But I find that this one does more often than not. Pisces love to please. Sometimes they smother. Leos love to be pleased. Too much adoration is never enough for the Lion. Therefore, as long as the Pisces doesn't fall into their famous "pity-parties" and accept the role of martyr, this combination could prove worthy despite what astrology books suggest. Both signs are romantic to the core, creative and enjoy sharing fantasies. It is worth mentioning that Leo needs to be extra sensitive to Pisces' emotional natures.

Leo with Aries—The no-compete clause needs to be included in the marriage contract between these two. Other than that, things can work out fine. Both have the fire and excitement to excel in life. If Leo will allow Aries the floor every now and then, things flow smoother. These over-achievers can amass nice fortunes and reputations. They can build a beautiful life for themselves. Both need to slow down long enough to enjoy it! Sex and romance will be a high-energy experience between these two fiery signs. As long as they put one another first in life, this union can last. Leo needs to sit atop the throne and Aries high on their pedestals.

Leo with Taurus—Leo natives could easily get stuck in Taurus' rut, experiencing the same old patterns and situations on a daily basis. The sameness makes the Bull feel secure and content but Leo the Lion needs to live! Leo cannot force Taurus to do anything. Even a gentle nudge will be meet with a defiant stomp of the Bull's hoof. So why fight? Better to find someone else that lives to catch that brass ring. Taurus can offer Leo security and loyalty. But Leo needs more. These two signs seldom see eye-to-eye.

Leo with Gemini—The Twins add spark to the Lion's world. They offer many things to Leo in a working or romantic relationship. Gemini have a way with words. They instinctively know what to say and when to say it. Leo loves the praise and flattery Gemini showers them with. Gemini, in turn, reap the rewards of Leo's big heart. Since air fans fire, Gemini will help promote or sell Leo's ideas to the world. Gemini will help keep Leo's spirits up in time of crisis or despair. This is a wonderful combination, because it provides each sun sign with the ability to use their natural gifts: Gemini (communication), Leo (generosity). Travel, friends and the social scene are all interests both can enthusiastically share in the Leo/Gemini relationship.

Leo with Cancer—The issue of who's in charge will likely come up at some point in this relationship. The home is the Leo's castle. The Cancer makes the house a home. Leo needs to relinquish their authority to Cancer regarding the raising of children and other family matters. Leos generally ride the fast track in the career world. Because of this, the issue of relocation almost always comes up. It could be deadly to this union if Cancer refuses to move. (Cancers seldom move away from the city they were born or raised in.) Sometimes this combination will work, usually when both partners are involved in careers. The best bet at making this last is to own a family business. Both signs are financially savvy. Cancer is the premiere promoter and Leo, the hardest worker. This could lend itself to a successful partnership in more ways than one.

Virgo—The Virgin

August 24–September 23

I often joke with my Virgo clients about their search for mates.

While looking for love, Virgo note every detail, from the hair out of place to the hole in the sock. Don't think for one minute that anything you're trying to cover up will go unnoticed. True, Virgos can be choosy, but they also expect perfection from themselves. They are their own worst critic. Virgos are also down-to-earth, loyal and quite giving. Most know their spiritual path is one of service to others and perform their job quite well. Virgos are likely to choose service-oriented professions such as medicine, hairdressing, teaching or plumbing.

When it comes to relationships, nothing is ever half way. There are the Virgos who hold out for years waiting for the perfect mate. Thus, the theory that most old maids are Virgos. Then there's the other type of Virgo: The one that consistently draws the sick puppies and the lost souls. It's as if they have stamped on their forehead, "Here to Serve and Save!"

Virgos are notorious for drawing mates who appear to be the "strong, perfect" partner. Then after a while, they found out these partners aren't so perfect after all. Poor Virgo, here to serve and save, stays in the negative, restricting relationship longer than they should.

Virgos are good at analyzing things. They have strong, quick minds but tend to worry too much. Sometime they drive their own selves crazy, dissecting things over and over in their minds. Virgos can do the same to their partners, too, if they are not careful. They just can't help it. They want to make sure you are healthy and happy and it's nice to know someone out there cares. Virgo is the most under ap- preciated sign of the zodiac. All of their nagging, nit picking and analyzing is really just a part of how they love. They may not make their partner's life completely perfect but they will certainly give their best while trying.

Virgo with Virgo—This relationship could grow quite dull. It feels like living with your brother or sister, rather than your lover. In this type of relationship, leading a life outside of the union is highly favored for survival. One must have a fulfilling career, friends and social activities to avoid that trapped or tied-down feeling. There is not much excitement in the home although together they could analyze one another for hours.

Virgo with Libra—The Virgo's impeccable taste can help dress the Libra for all of their grand social events. Libra will gently push the reserved Virgo out into that lively social scene. The two can learn much from one another if they will- ing to step into each other's world. This is not a match made in heaven, but sometimes it works when the partners accept the other for who they really are. Communication between the two is usually favorable as Libras intellectualize while Virgos analyze.

Virgo with Scorpio—Scorpio's hypnotic eyes will first attract Virgos but it's their intriguing mind that keeps the Virgin interested. Scorpio will help Virgo loosen up in the bedroom too, shedding sexual inhibitions and introducing Virgo to a more intense, passionate type of love. When Scorpio goes into their quiet, moody mode, Virgo may upset the apple cart by analyzing their condition and assuming something is wrong. Let Scorpio alone for a little while. Give them the space and isolation they so desperately need. Scorpio naturally knows how to "tune you out," so keep the nagging at a minimum. Learn when to step back, Virgo, and this relationship could last a lifetime.

Virgo with Sagittarius—You won't find this relationship combination in the majority and for good reason. It just doesn't work well. Virgo takes action in precise ways. Sagittarius throws caution to the wind and lives on faith. This couple may never see eye-to-eye. They may not be able to live under the same roof. Virgos keep their homes clean, tidy and in impeccable order. The Sagittarius residence resembles the morning after an all-night frat party. While Sag is living in the moment, Virgo is a step ahead, planning for their future. This will scare the freedom-loving Sag who makes no permanent commitments of any kind. However, there could be interesting debates between the two. Unfortunately they usually turn into arguments with the Sag bolting for the nearest exit door.

Virgo with Capricorn—These two sun signs are easily drawn to one another. Virgo's down-to-earth approach to life and Capricorn's cautious nature are in harmony. Simple pleasures are enjoyed and both know the value of a dollar. Home, family and traditions will play big roles in this partnership. Virgo will teach Capricorn how to "loosen up" and relax. There will be mutual respect and shared interests. Quiet evenings and weekends at home will be favored over crowded social events. Capricorn will appreciate Virgo's thriftiness and bargain-hunting abilities. They can depend on each other. Outsiders may see this relationship as dull and boring. But to the Capricorn and the Virgo, it's comfortable and safe, just the way they like it.

Virgo with Aquarius—Just when Virgo thinks things are settling down in this relationship and there's been a meeting of the minds, Aquarius is demanding new changes and wants to try new things. Aquarius, are always in a state of mid-life crisis. Both partners are intelligent people. Communication can be a strong point. Virgo needs to settle in one place, however, to build their perfect little world. Meanwhile, Aquarius want to explore the entire universe. Virgo cannot be supportive of Aquarius' constant need for change and challenge. Settling down is what Virgos do best. Aquarius will never settle. They are always veering off the beaten path, open to new developments and technology. Too many changes, relocations and abrupt career moves may cause major stress between these two.

Virgo with Pisces—This combination lends itself well to romance. Yet, Virgo and Pisces strike a nice balance between romantic love and everyday responsibilities. Both signs play the role of martyr very well. It's important to realize no one really needs to be saved. Too much smothering and mothering is not good. Individual growth is a must to keep the relationship alive. Often Virgo becomes Pisces' therapist and later resents Pisces if they do not follow the advice given. Pisces could also become too dependent on Virgo for basic needs. The less baggage these sun signs bring into the relationship, the easier it is.

Virgo with Aries—Since Virgos are apt to think first and act later, they often do not agree with Aries' "throw caution to the wind" attitude. Aries is a Fire sign. They just act upon their natural impulses and pay the consequences later. Aries do not have time or patience to wait around for Virgo to analyze all the little idiosyncrasies of life. Initially, these two could be drawn together because of their brilliant minds, but the long haul is going to be tedious for both signs.

Virgo with Taurus—Taurus will respect Virgo and appreciate the little things they do. Virgo will delight in having a partner on the same wavelength. These two could spend many happy years together. There is mutual understanding of how life works. But Virgo may anger Taurus if they nag too much about the Bulls' diet and weight. Taurus take pleasure in eating! Most Bulls have to be very careful about acquiring the middle age spread. Virgos are into the nutrition thing, but Taurus will resist any push or even a gentle nudge away from the dinner table. These two earth signs do have the ability to forge a deep solid bond and are considered one of the more compatibility connections in the zodiac.

Virgo with Gemini—Both have quick wits and pleasing personalities. They will find plenty to talk about and share a sense of humor. This combo works great for friendships, but for love, something seems to be missing. There is an undercurrent in the relationship that something is not right. Day to day, things will not flow smoothly. There is always an issue, a crisis or something that needs to be dealt with. Virgo may feel like everything rests on their shoulder, taking responsibility for all that is wrong in the relationship. Often Virgo and Gemini work at opposite ends to achieve the same means. Just be friends, Virgo. Life will be much easier that way.

Virgo with Cancer—If Virgo can learn to curb their helpful criticism and tiptoe around sensitive Cancer emotions, things can work out wonderfully. Together, these two can build a dream home, complete with the love, security and financial dreams they both will work hard for. There is a protective quality to this commitment. Each will look after the other, fussing as they go. If Cancer falls into one of their famous moods and clams up, Virgo can draw the crab out of their shell with a sense of humor. If Virgo is in crisis, Cancer offers a strong shoulder to lean on. This relationship grows even better with time.

Virgo with Leo—There could be instant attraction between these two, but it seldom lasts. Virgo will grow tired of Leo's boastful ways. Leo will expect Virgo to follow, to serve and take orders. Virgo doesn't mind fulfilling this role but needs to feel appreciated for their efforts. Leo can be too flashy and unorganized for the reserved Virgo. Virgo can help organize Leo's busy life, but often there is no time in it for the relationship itself. As long as Virgo agrees to play the role of the loyal and dependable worker, the relationship works. Once Virgo gives their two-week notice, it's over for good.

Libra—The Scales

September 24—October 23

Libras' purpose in life is to learn from relationships. Not, just those of a romantic nature, but most Libras think their life has little meaning unless they are in love. One of Libras' biggest lessons is to learn about balance in their world. If they put all of their energy into their relationship, they have no outside life. They miss out on the many other experiences the world has to offer them. If they swing the other way and, for instance, make career a top priority, they have no romance. To a Libra, an existence without wine and roses is like Christmas without presents! They must incorporate this balance in their life to be truly happy.

Libras are ruled by the planet Venus and are undoubtedly some of the most attractive people. They have strong creative natures and make excellent artists, writers and salespeople. Many Libras enter the law field as they believe strongly in fairness and justice. If someone is being mistreated, it is usually a Libra that will speak up and defend the victim. In love, Libras tend to bend to keep peace and harmony in the home. They hate confrontation. They will avoid it at any cost, even to their own detriment.

When looking for a mate, Libras have high standards. They are searching for that perfect person they have dreamed about since childhood. Seldom do they meet many who can fill the bill. So Libras need to bring their unrealistic views of love and romance down a notch in order to be satisfied. If they refuse, they will surely be disappointed time and time again.

Their easy-going and trusting nature makes them susceptible to liars and con artists, so they need to be careful whom they allow into their lives.

Once committed, the social Libra will still like to party. Thus, it's important they choose a partner who is not jealous and offers the freedom they need to express their fun-loving side.

These romantic creatures then will make wonderful mates who will add sparkle, joy and a sense of beauty to the lives of those they love.

Libra with Libra—The honeymoon never ends! Libra and Libra make a beautiful couple. However there's a strong inclination to party or socialize too much, which could lead to financial pitfalls. Harmony in the home life is strong. The two will be the envy of family and friends. Often this couple chooses not to have children, content with just the marriage. If they have a family, it is not a large one. The focus is strictly on the couple's relationship. They identify with one another. This couple believes strongly in the theory of soul mates.

Libra with Scorpio—Libra will be drawn to Scorpio almost instantly. They will find Scorpio a wonderful lover but eventually feel overwhelmed by their jealous and possessive personality. Scorpio will demand that Libra cut their many social ties. Libra will find they are constantly bending to keep the peace. They will walk on eggshells so as not to upset the brooding Scorpio, thus setting bad patterns in the union. When Libra has been pushed to their limit, they will finally stand up for themselves. When all else fails, they will leave. This relationship works short-term on a purely sexual level. Long term, it's not likely to last.

Libra with Sagittarius—Libra is looking for a commitment. Sagittarius is looking for something a little less permanent. This combination still holds promise. If the Sag is settled, mature and ready to put down roots, then Libra is a good choice for marriage. If not, Sag will wine and dine the Libra but ultimately disappoint. Size up the Sagittarius before your proceed, dear Libra. That way you won't be setting yourself up for a fall. These two could enjoy just being together. The two movie buffs could have a lot in common. The match makes for a great friendship too!

Libra with Capricorn—This sometimes works. I am more inclined to advise clients to look to other combinations for a more satisfying relationship. Libra is likely to find Capricorn boring. Libra will enjoy the financial rewards of being with the Goat, but the lovemaking may not be as passionate as they would like. Libra needs romance. Capricorn is very logical when it comes to the matters of the heart. The Libra wife cries, "You don't love me!" The Capricorn husband replies, "I pay the mortgage, the car insurance and the light bill. That proves I love you!" Capricorn is too busy with work to indulge in the vacations and parties Libra enjoys. They usually don't grow together, mostly apart.

Libra with Aquarius—Two highly intellectual people. This couple can understand the need for change and are open to it. Sometimes Aquarius can be a little too cool and aloof for Libra's romantic side. The Water Bearer is not one to whisper sweet nothings into the air. But Libra can help draw their deeply buried sensitive side to the surface. There will always be something to talk about between these two. Plans for the future are discussed early on in the relationship. It's as if they both know they've found the right one.

Libra with Pisces—Romantic love can be found here. Long-term compatibility is another story. Libra adores the dreamy Pisces. The affair seems like a romance novel filled with Pisces' flowery words and kisses. When the last chapter is read, reality sits in. Libra hangs on trying to recapture what once was. Pisces gets too comfortable. The Piscean pity parties start. They whine about everything! It could prove too much for the peace-loving Libra to bear. This couple can dream big beautiful dreams together, but seldom do they live them.

Libra with Aries—Libra is willing to let Aries lead. That's one of the main reasons this match has staying power. These two genuinely like each other. Libra doesn't fuss about Aries flirting with everyone in town because they are too busy doing the same thing. It's usually harmless fun. When dating, Libra feels emotionally needy toward the Aries. Upon marriage, they become strong, self-reliant confident mates. Libra is the one sign that can twist even the strongest Aries around their little finger. Libras' undying devotion gives Aries the reassurance they need that they are truly special. Aries, in turn, showers Libra with their own brand of love and affection. Doesn't everyone need to feel special?

Libra with Taurus—Both ruled by the planet Venus, Libra and Taurus will enjoy many of the same luxuries in life: fine art, music, wine, food and a lavish home. Taurus, however, will not agree with the way Libra spends their money. Libra will feel Taurus is a tightwad. It's Wednesday evening. Taurus want a quiet, early dinner at home. Libra wants to go dancing until the wee hours of the morning. They have some of the same likes, but their personality types may clash. Taurus will be jealous of the time Libra spends with friends. The possessive Taurean nature may be too much for Libra to handle. At some point Libra will ask, "What is more important—financial security or personal freedom?"

Libra with Gemini—The creative natures of the Libra and Gemini bring sexual and intellectual stimulation to this relationship. These folks work together well in business and in love, because they know how to communicate. Both love fun! They can be kids at heart and often look younger than their ages reveal. There is a possible warning for Libra. Gemini is a great used car salesman. Since Libra is prone to drawing con artists and manipulators, they need to exercise caution! Do not judge a book by its cover. This is not to say that Gemini can't be trusted. Just dig a little deeper, Libra, before you wear your heart on your sleeve. Once you feel comfortable and safe, there is no stopping the great heights this relationship can rise to. This could be the very relationship you've been waiting for!

Libra with Cancer—I am amazed at how many marriages I see carrying this sun sign combination. The Libra complains a lot about the Cancer's moodiness. Cancer feels the Libra is being unsupportive. Children will keep the union together longer but make no guarantee for a 50th wedding anniversary. It's best to address issues in this relationship as they come up, rather than letting them smolder beneath the surface. Big blow-ups leave Libra running to cry on their friend's shoulder and Cancer the Crab retreating into their shell.

Libra with Leo—This combination works better if the male is Leo. If the Libra lady is appropriately taken care of by her Leo mate, the relationship can be "all that." Libra appreciates the finer things in life. Leo's generous spirit and great financial savvy could provide the Libra with her lap of luxury. Libra, in turn, will make the Lion feel like the true king he is. There will be parties, mutual friends, exotic vacations and passionate lovemaking. If the Libra is the male partner in this scenario, he may often feel he is living in the Leo's grander shadow. The Leo woman will be generous but may prefer a more aggressive partner.

Libra with Virgo—Strong family and friendship ties usually remain strong between these two signs. Love and marriage is unlikely unless it serves a financial purpose. Libra's indecisive nature will drive Virgo up the wall. Time is valuable to Virgos and should not be wasted. Yet, Virgo will listen contentedly to Libra talk hour after hour about how their day went. These two signs have great minds. But it is their values that may differ. Libra will not sweat the small stuff. They look at the big picture. Virgos, on the other hand scrutinize every detail. They must have all angles covered before they step out into traffic. This could be a very frustrating and time-consuming relationship.

Scorpio—The Scorpion

October 23–November 22

The Scorpio is the most intense sign of all the zodiac. A relationship with a Scorpio will change your life forever. These folks are a force to be reckoned with.

You'd never know it at first glance. Scorpio seems so laid back and easy going. Maybe even a little bit shy. You'd think they couldn't hurt a fly. That's what they want you to think. They're sizing you up. Scorpio's poker face doesn't give away their true feelings but their eyes do. If you happen across a pair of penetrating, hypnotic eyes, the ones that draw you, from across a room, there's a Scorpio in your midst.

Seldom do they let any emotion show unless they are extremely angry. Scorpio natives are very controlled. They like to maintain control in their relationships, too. It makes them feel safe.

They trust no one, as they are suspicious and sometimes paranoid beings. You must earn a Scorpio's trust. Once you do, you will have a loyal comrade forever. They are hard to get to know but worth making the effort. They will be your dearest friend or boldest lover. If you cross them, they will be your worst enemy. I tell all of my clients, never fight a Scorpio, at work, in love or in any situation. You will end up on the losing end. Motto to live by: The Scorpio's way or the highway.

They are the best at mind games, known to be master manipulators and usually end up getting their way, one way or another.

Scorpio has gained a sexy reputation. They are known to be the best lover among the sun signs. They view sex as power and also as the only way to release those emotions they hold so close to their heart.

Many are healers, doctors and researchers. They have brilliant, analytical minds. Scorpio is the one sign that can be at the bottom of the barrel in the game of life and rise straight to the top. Anything they desire they can manifest, if it is for their highest good.

In love, they are intense, deeply wounded when hurt, and they can be revengeful. But when they completely open their heart and learn to trust, a relationship with a Scorpio can be an intense spiritual experience like no other. The Scorpio will sense your needs, touch your heart and then capture your soul.

Scorpio with Scorpio—These two have the ultimate sex life! There is great financial power with this couple. There will be control issues to contend with and some knock-'em down, drag 'em-out fights. Let's hope these two don't use Voodoo dolls when they're angry! Money and sex will keep this relationship going through the hard times. The good times will be filled with family ties, special private moments, traveling, acquiring property and career advancements.

Scorpio with Sagittarius—A sexy fling may be all that comes of this match-up. Sag wants freedom while Scorpio wants to possess. The first few dates would be great, but the momentum would eventually dwindle. This is not a relationship Sagittarius could easily pop in and out of, like they do with other signs. Scorpio wants all or nothing. You've been properly warned, Sag!

Scorpio with Capricorn—Sexual attraction is strong. Scorpio feels safe with Capricorn. They will argue because Capricorn holds very strong opinions on all subject matters. It is hard for Capricorn to imagine anyone could hold a differing opinion. Surprisingly, these two can kiss and make up quicker after an argument than any of the other signs. They can communicate well. The financial picture should be a bright one. This has all of the makings of a long-term relationship.

Scorpio with Aquarius—Scorpio is too smart to pursue Aquarius. They would irritate one another. There would be constant bickering. Aquarius is not into mind games or submission. The only way for this type of relationship to maintain itself is for the partners to take separate vacations, work long hours and claim different residences (preferably on opposite ends of the country). This is one of the more difficult matches, and I would avoid even thinking of going down this road.

Scorpio with Pisces—These two water signs complement each other. Pisces will be very helpful and caring towards the Scorpio. These natives are like sponges. They tend to soak in other people's problems and feelings. This is not good because Pisces could easily take on the Scorpio's woes. Pisces also smother their loved ones and Scorpio has a deep need for intervals of isolation. They could resent Pisces crowding their space. If the Pisces is a strong personality, this pair can weave magic into their every day lives. If Pisces is weak, the Fish will carry most of life's everyday load alone.

Scorpio with Aries—Most Scorpios don't find Aries to their liking. They can see through Aries' little mind games and power plays right away. At times, sexual sparks fly, but by the time they dance around one another, nothing gets off the ground. Jealous Scorpio will not stand for Aries flirting with others. The time and energy spent on trying to make this relationship work is not worth the end result. Infidelity, money, and control issues will come up again and again. Trust, or the lack of it, will be a big problem.

Scorpio with Taurus—"I've met my match," cries the delighted Scorpio. Taurus' sexual drive is almost as strong as Scorpio's. These two hard headed, jealous, possessive signs will bring out the best in one another. They expect the same things from their mate: loyalty, devotion, and fidelity. They will succeed in attaining great financial fortune if they work together. Both will probably keep secret bank accounts in their own names because of their controlling nature, but joint resources will grow over the years giving the couple the security they so desire. These two have bad tempers but express them quite differently. The Taurus temper builds up and erupts like a massive volcano. Then it simmers back down. Scorpio will be more secretive, plotting out their revenge with a smile upon their face. If this couple can learn not to take the little arguments so seriously, this relationship could last a lifetime.

Scorpio with Gemini—This relationship doesn't have staying power. Most of the time, these two signs aren't even attracted to one another. The Scorpio's intensity is too overwhelming for flighty Gemini. Once in a blue moon, you may hear of such a combination but seldom in my practice, does the issue of the Scorpio and Twin ever come up.

Scorpio with Cancer—These emotional, psychic signs know just the right thing to say or do to lift each other's spirits. If they are both depressed at the same time, we have quite a problem! The relationship will be centered around the family and building their own traditions. Scorpio and Cancer have photographic minds. They don't miss anything. It's important that they fight fair and agree to peace treaties. Issues not resolved could come up years later. Both are excellent at manipulating situations to their benefit. They'd run a great family business. Scorpio has to be careful that their stinging criticism doesn't hurt the Crab, while Cancers need to learn not to take things too personally.

Scorpio with Leo—Scorpio can only take so much of the Lion. Many times Scorpions find they just don't like the kind of energy Leo gives out. This relationship will have more than its share of emotional outbursts and power struggles. Royal Leo roars, "I am your King". Scorpio bows to no one. There's a mixing of fire and water here. Leo may think they are winning this battle but Scorpio will ultimately win the war, even if it means the death of the relationship.

Scorpio with Virgo—This type of relationship usually starts out as a friendship and develops over time. If it leads to commitment, Scorpio and Virgo will settle down nicely. Arguments are likely to be over little silly things that don't seem so silly at the time. Scorpio will resort to the silent-treatment tactic, and Virgo will try to analyze the root of the problem. The best antidote for a happier marriage between the two is not to sweat the small stuff. Most of the time this combination works great. But Virgo must accept the fact that living with any Scorpio is never easy.

Scorpio with Libra—Here is mutual admiration and attraction but the fireworks don't last. Scorpio would be able to control Libra and eventually realize there is no test or challenge in this relationship. Scorpios are not afraid of confrontation. Libra runs from it. Sometimes when things are running smoothly in a relationship, Scorpio will try and stir the pot a little, just to cause some friction. The relationship seems more exciting to them that way. More importantly, they'll get the chance to kiss and make up!

Sagittarius—The Archer

November 23–December 22

These are the Don Juans of the zodiac. Both the Sagittarius men and women are some of the most charming people you'll ever meet. Sagittarius women are more thoughtful, however, when it comes to breaking off restrictive relationships than men are. Most Sag men think it nothing to date several women at the same time. They are notoriously known for their little black books.

Sag men are like little boys to the women who love them. So they tend to get away with the most inexcusable behavior. They know how to dish out the compliments, and make their women feel as if they are truly princesses. Women swoon over them all the time. They have the worst pick-up lines but know how to make them work. Their biggest fear is settling down. A Sagittarius man will marry well into his forties, if at all.

The Sagittarius woman is strong, poised and brutally honest. She will play counselor to all of her friends. Yet, she hates to burden others with her own troubles. She is optimistic and happy. People love to be around her. She is looking for a mate who can also be her best friend.

Communication is a must in any affair with a Sag woman. If her mate will not talk to her, the relationship is not going to work. Many Sag women prefer dating younger men and enjoy hanging out with the guys. Most of their guy friends are secretly in love them!

Sagittarius men and women are lucky. They seem to get out of sticky situations with ease and have a extra guardian angel hovering over their shoulders.

When they do settle down, they never settle. They make sure their partners will give them the encouragement they need and the freedom to be themselves. Even after marriage some Sagittarius will keep their romantic options open.

They make excellent real estate tycoons, gamblers, athletes, lawyers, travel agents and international diplomats.

To love a Sagittarius is an adventure like no other. You must have a strong heart, an open mind and be ready to let the good times roll!

Sagittarius with Sagittarius—If their brutal honesty doesn't kill the relationship, the two Archers may have a good thing. If the relationship is not working, both have the sense to move on to greener pastures without hesitation and long overdrawn good-byes. Usually the couple can work almost any problems through because of their positive natures. "Nothing is as bad as it seems", and "Tomorrow is another day" are mottoes Sagittarius live by. Sports, travel, spiritual pursuits and gambling may be some of the pastimes these couples will enjoy.

Sagittarius with Capricorn—Sagittarius fight to break the very structure and traditions Capricorn work to build. The two may enjoy each other's company and no-nonsense approach to life, but there is no place for the freedom-loving Sagittarius in Capricorn's organized world. Sag wouldn't want to live there too long anyway. There are too many places to see, people to meet and hearts to conquer. Capricorn will never understand the Sagittarius wanderlust, but they will secretly envy it. This is not a "till death do we part" kind of love.

Sagittarius with Aquarius—Here we have two freedom-and-truth seekers who don't mind abrupt changes sweeping them off in new directions. They both hate to be tied down and will try anything once. Sagittarius and Aquarius is a great match! They will talk about spiritual paths and learn to meditate together. Aquarius expects loyalty. So if the Sagittarius is really ready to make that kind of commitment, Aquarius should jump at the chance. Their life together will be one of great exploration!

Sagittarius with Pisces—The negative side of the Pisces is going to hurt the chances of a long-lasting relationship with Sagittarius. The optimistic Archer wants to hear only the happy stories in life and not be burdened with crisis. Pisces' will feel they're getting no support from Sag during the hard times. Pisces constant smothering will give Sagittarius justification for leaving the relationship. The two will not see eye-to-eye much. Pisces may not accept reality and try to win the Sagittarius back long after the break-up. These couples are the type that end up on the Jerry Springer Show.

Sagittarius with Aries—While some signs may find Aries too aggressive and bold for their tastes, Sagittarius adores what Aries can bring to a relationship. The Archer and the Ram find much to gab about. They agree that one should take risks and that nothing is impossible. If they choose to commit, they will find sexual compatibility, and they will share a love for knowledge and higher education. They will allow one another to take turns playing the role of teacher and student. Travel, shopping and fast cars will be some of their life's pleasures.

Sagittarius with Taurus—Sagittarius' charm draws the Taurus but there's not much else to hold this relationship together for long. When the Bull's possessive side comes charging out, Sag will have no choice but to run. Sag favors their personal freedom over the financial security Taurus can offer, although they'd like to keep both. But if it came right down to it, Sag isn't going to let anyone fence them in. The famous Taurus temper is also something Sagittarius will not tolerate. Money making ventures would be highly profitable between the two, but I wouldn't gamble a dime on the relationship working out.

Sagittarius with Gemini—The Archer and the Twins take their time getting to the altar. There's no rush to settle down, according to these two. By the time "I do's" are exchanged, these signs often know exactly what they want in a committed relationship. As long as they both remain faithful to each other, Sagittarius and Gemini could enjoy a blessed union. They would be supportive of one another's goals. The communication lines are always open. The two share many of the same interests and hobbies. Both love to bargain-shop. Besides being lovers, Sag and Gemini could be best of friends. Go for it!

Sagittarius with Cancer—Their souls connect. Their eyes meet. They are drawn to one another across the crowded room. The Sagittarius/Cancer love affair offers romance novel-writers great material. However, this couple would be better off reading the book than living it. Most of these connections don't end happily ever after. This is very confusing because the initial attraction is so strong. Sag and Cancer are like two magnets. They can't stay away from one another. Eventually, the Crab's need to settle down will suffocate the freedom-loving Archer. Arguments are par for the course. The relationship is on and off for months, even years, until they realize it doesn't meet their individual needs.

Sagittarius with Leo—These sun sign natives love to have fun. They will live for the moment and dream big!

This is a relationship that would never get dull. Money making ventures and business deals prove lucky. However, they both need to be cautious about gambling too much. The fun could turn into an addiction. There are usually no complaints in the bedroom. Leo will need to curb their bossy tendencies. Sag needs to be gentle with Leo's ego. The biggest concern is overindulgence. Leo and Sagittarius do nothing halfway. It's usually to the extreme. They believe in living life to the fullest and often on the edge!

Sagittarius with Virgo—Let's look at a ordinary week in the life of Sagittarius and Virgo. There are seven days in the week. The first three days are just wonderful. Things run smoothly. The couple is in love. They laugh. They talk. Then the fourth day hits. It's downhill from here. Little arguments start. They pick on one another. They can't stand to be in the same room. The battle lines are drawn. The less time these two spend together, the longer the relationship will last. It's that simple. Too much togetherness will mean the death of this union. Personalities clash and defenses go up. It would be best to avoid this connection.

Sagittarius with Libra—Many times in a Sagittarius/Libra relationship, there is what appears to be a permanent breakup. More often than not, this couple gets a second chance. Sag is hard to tie down. They need to get their wanderlust out of their system before they make a lifetime commitment. Libra, on the other hand, has been wait-ing for the church bells to ring all of their life. These two can enjoy a great relationship. But the timing has to be right. When Sag has filled all of life's curiosities, they will likely come back for Libra. Hopefully, Sagittarius won't make Libra wait too long.

Sagittarius with Scorpio—Usually crisis brings couples closer together. In the Sagittarius/Scorpio relation-ship, crisis could pull them apart. This relationship will have more than its share of problems. Each sun sign deals with problems in different ways. Scorpio want answers immedi-ately. They are intense and emotional personalities. Sagittarius is apt to take a more carefree, lighthearted approach to issues. Thus, Scorpio feels Sagittarius doesn't really care. Issues of jealousy, fidelity and money will likely come up. There is pas-sion, but the flames may die out if Scorpio's emotional needs don't get met too.

Capricorn—The Goat

December 23–January 20

Capricorns are cautious when it comes to love. It may take them months, and sometimes years to ask for a date. It is important they know they won't be turned down. When they do finally get around to falling in love, they mean serious business. When they do date, the event is impeccably planned out, far in advance.

Capricorns look for partners they can feel proud of. Traditionalists, at heart, they often search for a loyal, marriage-minded mate with financial savvy. Social status is very important to them. This is not to say, Capricorns are snobby, they just like to be respected by others. They are serious-type creatures. Emotional people scare them, although Capricorns tend to draw to them what they lack. Many find commitments among the feeling water signs: Pisces, Cancer and Scorpio.

Capricorns are hard workers. Some are workaholics. They strive for money and the status it can bring. They can be firm with their children, perhaps a little too rigid but their children will never go without. They make sure their off springs have the best they can afford.

Romance is not high on their list of priorities but sex is. Some born under the sign send mixed signals to their partner. Their logical, stoic personality doesn't always lend itself to romance. But they can be very convincing when sexually attracted to someone.

These are the strong, dependable types. They also don't bend easily. Their one-sided opinions discourage communication with their mates. They are not as bull-headed as the Taurus or as unyielding as Scorpio, but Cappys will stand their ground if the cause is right. They are very direct people, too. Sometimes others, with sensitive souls, find them downright rude. Capricorns speak their mind. They don't hold much back. If you ask a question, expect a honest, direct answer.

Marriage is for life, according to the Capricorn. They will work hard to provide the worldly comforts for their family. In crisis, they're the strong people who help others through adversities. Honor, tradition and stability are what the Capricorn has to offer in a relationship. If you're not into all of that mushy stuff, the goat will make a wonderful partner!

Capricorn with Capricorn—Both career driven individuals, this couple will have to set aside time to see one another. The great wealth they could accumulate is undeniable, but arguments could arise about how to spend it. The earlier years of the commitment/marriage will be filled with hard work, juggling family and career along with the normal squabbles. In later years, the craziness starts. Capricorns mature earlier then most other signs. Therefore, they miss out on enjoying their teenage and young adult years. After middle age sets in, they realize they want to live the childhood they never had. They can act irrationally. Marriages can feel restricting. It's important that during the mid-life crisis, the couple balance their new ideas with the traditions they've established in the past for their lives to run smoothly.

Capricorn with Aquarius—The Aquarius new-age ideals will clash with the traditional ways of the Capricorn. Aquarius seeks change and is constantly looking toward the future. Capricorn hangs on tightly to the past and does not easily accept change. This couple's tastes are worlds apart. The Goat favors the Rolex watch, the Gucci suit and designer glasses. The Water Bearer may sport the latest fads: tattoos, body piercing, and the cool hairdo, complete with purple highlights!

Capricorn with Pisces—Pisces will help Capricorn understand and escape into their subconscious. They will open their world to dreams, romance and fantasy. It will take a little nudging on the part of the Fish, but Capricorn will find the Pisces personality a nice retreat after a hard day at the office. Pisces will help the Capricorn to relax and not look at the world too seriously. Their spirits can intertwine. Generally, this combination works if the couple looks at one another as equals.

Capricorn with Aries—Things move too fast in this relationship for Capricorn. Cappy doesn't approve of Aries' pushy, impractical attitude. Aries doesn't want to wait for anything! Their pioneering spirit forces them to make drastic changes on the spur of the moment. Aries is too much for Capricorn to handle. The cautious Goat needs to think before making a decision. Aries doesn't have time to sit around. They need to take action! One partner is always a step ahead or a step behind the other.

Capricorn with Taurus—These two earth signs have what it takes to make a relationship work. Their basic needs are the same. They are actually quite alike. There will be arguments over money. Security-driven Taurus expects to handle all of the finances. Organized Capricorn thinks they're the best for the job. Separate bank accounts may be a good idea for these two. Hardworking Capricorn may find Taurus a little lazy when it comes to work around the house. Other than that, the relationship is very comfortable.

Capricorn with Gemini—Since Capricorn represents the mature, responsible, old sign of the zodiac, they don't connect well with Gemini, the youthful, fun-loving sign. They can offer one another a fresh, new way of looking at things. Flexible Gemini will be more than happy to share their ideas. However, Capricorn is very opinionated and may feel Gemini's views are just a waste of their valuable time.

Capricorn with Cancer—A case of opposites attract. Cancer could make the most magnificent home for Capricorn, complete with all of the family traditions and loyalties Capricorn is so attached to. Capricorn can supply Cancer with the financial security they need. The problems arise when logical Capricorn does not take Cancer's supersensitive feelings into consideration. The cold exterior of the Capricorn doesn't melt for many, but Cancer is the one sign that has the capability to soften the Goat up.

Capricorn with Leo—The goat and the lion can be workaholics. They often work long days and take any overtime passed their way. They identify themselves by what they do for a living. How they spend their paychecks is quite a different story. Leo thinks Capricorn is a tightwad with money. Capricorn feels Leo should be put on a restricted allowance so they don't blow it all Saturday night. There is some truth to both beliefs. Capricorn is happy to spend nights and weekends at their lovely home. Leo enjoys family but likes to be the social butterfly and often is in the spotlight. Leo's flashy style clashes with Capricorn's more reserved attitudes. Anything more than a business partnership may not last.

Capricorn with Virgo—The Capricorn/Virgo relationship works like a charm. Their lives will be organized, orderly, conservative and a bit boring. This is the couple that will have their mortgage paid off, kids married and a great retirement program set up by age fifty. They work together for the same things in life. They communicate on the same wavelength. Virgo's coupon-clipping abilities, will be admired by the Capricorn, who believes in saving for rainy days, too. The excitement in this couple's life comes from everything running smoothly.

Capricorn with Libra—Save yourself some time and money, Capricorn. Look elsewhere for love. On the surface, this relationship looks promising. Capricorn and Libra enjoy nice things, designer fashion and high social status. The couple will be at odds over their free time. Their hobbies and interests are different. Social Libra may want to party or dance all night long. Capricorn thinks early-to-bed, early-to-rise. If a balance is not struck between the two, they will go off in different directions.

Capricorn with Scorpio—Capricorn and Scorpio are private people. Reserved, quiet and sometimes, aloof, the couple comes alive in the bedroom. They enjoy each other's company and will work hard at any problems or crisis that comes up in a marriage. Concerns arise when Scorpio's emotional side is neglected. The Goat is very logical in love. Seldom do they bring flowers and candy. Capricorn needs to learn a shoulder to lean on is sometimes better than practical advice. Scorpio hears Capricorn say "I love you," but they need to feel it, too.

Capricorn with Sagittarius—This is not one of the best combinations for love. This relationship will have a short fuse. Since both signs enjoy a good debate, communication presents no problem for this pair but the physical attraction is not strong. Sagittarius breaks tradition too much for Capricorn to feel safe. Capricorns are always on time for their appointments and dates. They often arrive early. Sagittarius is notoriously late. Their housekeeping habits would drive Capricorn up the wall. Sagittarius don't mind clutter. They're known to have messy bachelor pads. Tidy Capricorn has a place for everything. They are known for having the clean, organized closets. If these two decide to make a go of it, Capricorn will have to loosen up a little. Sagittarius will have to buy a watch!

Aquarius—The Water Bearer

January 21–February 19

Aquarius people are unique and eccentric individuals. They either irritate everyone around them or draw favor. Friendship is most important to people born under this sign. Many pull away from the families they were born into and make new families among their peer groups and acquaintances.

Because Aquarius get bored easily, they are constantly looking to change something in their lives. After a few years at a job, they grow tired of the same old working conditions. They may adore their home but give it up to move clear across the country.

Unfortunately, this holds true in the area of romance, too. Aquarius divorce more than any other sun sign. Multiple marriages are the norm.

Their cool, aloof nature may help contribute to divorce if they've drawn a needy partner.

Aquarius is the one sign that can appear to completely shut their feelings off. If you break off a relationship with an Aquarius, they will act like it's no big deal. If there's a crisis, they appear unnerved. They dismiss any feelings they have. They deny the pain. What they don't realize is that those suppressed feelings have to come out sometime. They could manifest in health problems or sudden outbursts of anger. Maybe the pain hurts too deeply so they can't bear to express it. It would help their relationships if they would.

Aquarius like the latest fads. They are into the new age, advanced technology and often find their niche working with computers. If you're surfing the web, there's bound to be an Aquarius in your chat room.

Many times you will find Aquarius spearheading fundraisers and causes. They enjoy large groups rather than an intimate relationship. They look for love among these fellow comrades.

The Aquarius men sometimes have a mean streak. They can be strong-willed and unbending. This often accounts for a childhood in which emotions were denied rather than nurtured. The majority of Aquarians I have counseled do not have a desire to have children. A family would hold them back from mothering the entire world. Aquarius' deepest desire is to make the world a better place.

The Aquarius women expect equality in a relationship. They will love intensely, but may search for years to find the perfect mate, as their needs are constantly changing.

The way to enjoy a relationship with an Aquarius is to let them be who they are. Don't try to change them. Support their goals and dreams. Most of all, be their best friend.

Aquarius with Aquarius—If both are working toward the same goals, this duo can expect great happiness. Think of all of the growth and spiritual development they will experience. They understand the need for change. Life will never be boring. This couple will try the latest foods, hair-styles and fads. Their home will be full of the latest gadgets and new technology. Pets will be treated like royal members of the family. Friends who drop by to visit could find the hospitality so inviting that they will stay way past their welcome. Politics, humanitarian efforts and the Internet will be shared interests.

Aquarius with Pisces—If this relationship gets past the first phone call or e-mail, then it has potential. The two communicate so differently. Pisces could find Aquarius condescending. Aquarius says Pisces is too shallow. The first date will lay the basis for who's in control of this relationship. If Aquarius takes over, Pisces will feel left out around all of Aquarius' friends. Pisces wants to explore their romantic dreams, and Aquarius is too technical when it comes to the theory of love. If Pisces takes the lead, Aquarius will soon grow bored, tired of the smothering, and Pisces' constant need for reassurance. Just be friends.

Aquarius with Aries—Here's a good gamble. Aries are willing to try anything once. They are strong and self-assured and have lots to say. Aquarius will appreciate the positive, upbeat personality of the Ram. When they argue, they will fight fair. Often, there will be no resolution because both signs are the know-it-alls of the zodiac. They can learn a lot from one another if they just listen. This will be one of the few relationships in which Aries will feel like someone is on their side. Aries demand to be number one. With Aquarius, they'll never have to ask for admiration or support. It'll be right there. In turn, Aries will encourage the Water Bearer to go after their wildest dreams.

Aquarius with Taurus—Disappointment will be no stranger to this relationship. Taurus and Aquarius are fixed signs. They don't bend easily. Taurus will not permit Aquarius to volunteer for every community effort in town. There's dinner to be made, bills to pay and the Taurus needs attention. Aquarius need the energy they draw from other people. They feel alive and connected to the universe when they are with their friends. Its important for Aquarius to know they are contributing to society in some way. Taurus don't relish change; Aquarius crave it. Sometimes differences in a relationship are healthy, but here they could prove otherwise.

Aquarius with Gemini—The energy between these two air signs flow nicely. They can talk nonsense for hours! If there's serious business to discuss, these quick minds will work together to get the job done. There's not much bickering here. Power struggles are few and far between. Friends are welcome any time day or night. This couple also would work well together in the areas of research or teaching. Attraction can last through the years because both are willing to pursue new ideas. Although the word "forever" isn't in either's vocabulary, Aquarius and Gemini do agree never to say "never."

Aquarius with Cancer—Some astrology books claim this relationship has its potential. In my practice, it has proved to be one of the most difficult to maintain and derive any pleasure from. The differences of the two sun signs produce attraction in the initial stage of romance. But Aquarius cannot give the moody Cancer the emotional security they need. Home and family-loving Cancer cannot give Aquarius the freedom to make sweeping changes in their lives. Both have completely different purposes to fulfill in this lifetime. It's very likely the things Cancer holds most dear, Aquarius usually are not interested in. I have seen major problems between these signs, whether the relationship consisted of romance, work or family. Friendships seem to be different. Aquarius treat their friends like Cancer would treat their family. Cancer and Aquarius—be friends!

Aquarius with Leo—Aquarius can be harmonious in relation to Leo. They are opposites but possess some of the same strong desires and goals. Both have big hearts but show them off them in different ways. The Leo heart will be generous when in love. They will shower the object of their affection with gifts and special attention. The Aquarius heart is big when it comes to helping the world. They give to the homeless, less fortunate and underprivileged. They can learn a lot from one another. Leo can learn that the power of love comes back when you give it away. The more people you touch, the more your life will be blessed. Aquarius can learn through Leo, that sharing begins in the home.

Aquarius with Virgo—Virgo will certainly make Aquarius more aware of their responsibilities in life. Aquarius don't care to hear about the mundane. But there are bills to pay! A Virgo woman will have a "honey do" list ready every weekend. Never mind if Aquarius has plans with his buddies. Virgo knows that more important things come first. They will bicker about money and household chores. The Virgo man will not approve of the Aquarius woman's funky fashion statements. He may try to squash her sense of style. Compromise is the only way this relationship can survive.

Aquarius with Libra—The potential for happiness is strong with these lovebirds. Libra won't argue like other signs when Aquarius needs to make drastic lifestyle changes. Just as long as Libra is part of those changes, all will be fine! The intellectual and creative energies these two possess is a turn-on. Libra can bring balance to Aquarius' erratic life. Friends are like family here, and socializing is a big part of their relationship.

Aquarius with Scorpio—The Aquarius can handle a demanding career, family and a couple of worthy causes. But it's unlikely they'll be able to handle the Scorpio. Don't even try, Aquarius. The intense Scorpio will not allow you to get your way. There'll be no lifestyle changes without their approval. Unless it's true love, don't waste the energy.

Aquarius with Sagittarius—What a delightful match! Aquarius and Sagittarius can enrich each other's lives. They have much to share. Both are determined to make the best of whatever it is that life hands them. They are willing to grab the brass ring and do it with such passion that it spills over into their relationship. The couple's calendar will be full with busy career activities and plans with friends. If Sagittarius has truly settled down, then expect longevity in this relationship. If not, the romance will be marked by highs and lows but undoubtedly will be a very special one.

Aquarius with Capricorn—The tried and true works well for the cautious Capricorn. The Aquarius want to try new things. There's a definite clash of ideas when they get together. Capricorn will not find the steadiness they are looking for in such a relationship. They must learn to expect the unexpected if they further this union. Aquarius could feel restricted in the commitment, never finding the freedom they seek necessary to be true to them selves.

Pisces—The Fish

February 20–March 21

If you meet someone with the most beautiful sea green or watery-blue eyes, you've probably met a Pisces.

Pisces believe in fairy tales with the happily-ever-after endings. They are the dreamers of the zodiac. They love to be in love. Fantasy plays a big part in their love life, which often leads to trouble or disappointment. Pisces are gentle, spiritual creatures that live to please their mates. They will go to the ends of the earth to make sure their lover is happy.

They are also very intuitive, and their dreams can be prophetic. I tell my Pisces clients to listen to their dreams and learn how to interpret them.

Pisces also are known to draw the losers and the lost souls. Often I see Pisces men and women in bad relationships that they can't seem to leave. They play the role of the martyr well, and some put up with years of abuse: mental, verbal, emotional and sometimes physical. They feel they can change things. But mostly, they feel guilt. Pisces carry the weight of the world on their backs. They feel guilty about everything. They feel sorry for everyone.

Once Pisces learn to deal with their guilt, they can begin the healing process: build their self-esteem and leave their negative relationships.

The Pisces, in a healthy relationship, prosper. They are

excellent business people and can attain a great deal of wealth.

All Pisces have a positive and negative side. When they get into their famous pity parties, they can stay there for weeks. Their tears turn on and run like a faucet.

If they deny their emotional feelings, they will need to be careful of using escapism to cope, such as drugs or alcohol. Some Pisces have a tendency to drink if depressed or overburdened.

Artistic and helpful, Pisces make great artists, counselors, hairdressers and business owners. They whine too much. They dream too much. Some say they love too much. That's not so terrible, now is it?

Pisces with Pisces—Pisces people are so indecisive that they frustrate themselves. They find it hard to make decisions because they see both sides to a situation and don't want to feel guilty if the make the wrong choice. If they ever make up their minds to walk down the aisle, what a romantic fairy tale they could tell. The truth is, Pisces live soap-opera lives. There is always a crisis or concern to overcome. The emotional roller coaster ride they would take together may never end! It would be better to settle with one of the earth signs— Taurus, Capricorn or Virgo—to help with grounding. But if they're sure they've found their soul mate, Pisces can dream big dreams together and live in romantic escape.

Pisces with Aries—Aries may grow tired of Pisces' incessant whining but they love the attention Pisces showers on them. As long as Pisces doesn't smother, Aries will look down from their pedestal with appreciation. This relationship benefits Aries more than Pisces in the long run, but the two can make a go of it if both parties share the responsibilities of commitment.

Pisces with Taurus—Taurus will need to watch their temper around sensitive Pisces, whose feelings could easily get bruised. But overall, this match works. Taurus need a lot of attention and affection. Pisces could smother and mother all they want! The Bull will help bring Pisces back down to earth when they are caught up in their dream world. If they can't make a decision, logical Taurus will make it for them. Worries are lifted! Romance, candlelight, fine wine and true love would last a lifetime for these two.

Pisces with Gemini—A dating relationship of this sort should not be taken too seriously. The Gemini would probably agree. If Pisces falls head over heels in love, there's danger ahead! Gemini's fickle nature and need for variety will bring Pisces great disappointment. The two could carry on brilliant conversations. Their creative minds work well together. But Pisces won't be able to see through their rose-colored glasses that a long-term commitment will not work.

The Fish may hang onto the relationship long after Gemini has moved on.

Pisces with Cancer—This pair would be worth betting on. Pisces and Cancer tend to get depressed more often than some of the other signs. Cancers can get quite moody around the full moon. Pisces are like sponges. They soak up everything in their environment. If the couple's moods are in harmony most of the time, the relationship works. If there are many emotional ups and downs, there will be problems. Their basic natures are to be caring, sympathetic and kind. If they bring these qualities out in one another, the union will prosper.

Pisces with Leo—Here's where Pisces can play their role very well. Pisces love to please and Leos love to be pleased. But it's a two-way street. Leos need to make sure they don't take Pisces for granted or they'll become a cold fish. Most astrologers say this is not a match made in heaven. I agree, but I have seen more cases that have worked out wonderfully. If there's mutual compassion, and both parties benefit, I like the idea.

Pisces with Virgo—These opposites could easily make things work if they took the time to listen more to each another. They actually make a pretty good team. Virgo will fuss over Pisces' health and Pisces will just fuss. Their home is apt to be filled with children, pets, extended families and chaos. Virgo like to help people and Pisces like to please people. This couple could run a successful business, working with the public. Things won't always run smooth. These folks tend to bite off more than they can chew, but it's workable.

Pisces with Libra—Both with indecisive minds, these sun signs would probably drive each other nuts, but they hate to offend. Pisces likes to stir up the pot every now and then. Libra hates confrontation. The upside to this union is the romance. But in the long run, the relationship could be frustrating and wear thin.

Pisces with Scorpio—Intense Scorpio may be too much for Pisces to handle over the long haul. The relationship has merit, though. Pisces indulge Scorpio in their wildest fantasies. Pisces' will also find Scorpio to be a strong ally in their corner during times of adversity and crisis. Scorpio's natural healing powers can soothe Pisces' worries and emotional ups-and-downs. If they are at odds, Scorpio's influence will not be a healthy one for Pisces' emotional well-being.

Pisces with Sagittarius—This is one of those relationships in which gullible, trusting Pisces could get hurt. If the Sagittarius is mature and has truly settled down, then the relationship will be strained at times but can work. If the Sagittarius is still seeking freedom, Pisces are likely to set themselves up for disappointment. Smothering in this type of relationship doesn't work for Pisces. It backfires. Freedom-loving Sag will not appreciate everything they do. This relationship could be very one-sided.

Pisces with Capricorn—The Capricorn could easily take on the role of parent in this relationship; with Pisces of course, being the child. If this happens, the relationship is doomed. It may last, but each partner will feel unfulfilled. It's best if each has a successful career, separate goals and interests to bring to the relationship. Mutual respect is a must for survival. The two should get along very well. This nice blend of a water and earth sign lends itself to even more compatibility. Stoic Capricorn may not always understand Pisces' strong, emotional nature but it helps to soften their hearts a little.

Pisces with Aquarius—Go ahead and meet for lunch, but I wouldn't agree to anything more than that. These two make better friends than lovers. They could ruin a wonderful friendship if they step over the line. Aquarius need their space. Pisces may take "extra space" as rejection. As a business team, they'd do well. Pisces' creative abilities, coupled with the Aquarian's technical brain, could invent or create a huge money making venture. But romance is likely to be a letdown.

CHAPTER FOURTEEN

Fun Facts on The Sun Signs

And the Award Goes To . . . Each zodiac sign has garnered reputations over the years for being the best or worst or "most likely to." Obviously, these monikers are not written in stone and not meant to offend, but here's an amusing compilation of sun sign statistics.

Best Lovers—Scorpio, Taurus

Don Juans—Sagittarius, Gemini, Aries

Marrying Types—Cancers, Taurus, Libra

Old Maid—Virgo

Most Bisexuals—Gemini, Pisces, Libra

FUN FACTS ON THE SUN SIGNS

Marry Later in Life—Sagittarius, Gemini

Most Divorced—Aquarius

Most Cheaters—Sagittarius, Gemini, Pisces

Most Kids, fertile signs—Cancer

Biggest Flirt—Aries

Biggest Heart—Leo

Most Revengeful—Scorpio

Most Romantic—Pisces, Cancer

Most Sexy—Scorpio, Sagittarius

Kinkiest—Scorpio

Plays Great Mind Games—Aries, Scorpio

Most Fickle—Gemini

Most Loyal—Virgo, Capricorn, Cancer

Most Jealous—Taurus, Scorpio

Most Possessive—Taurus

Most Sentimental—Cancer, Pisces

Most Old Flames Return to—Cancer

Dreamiest Eyes—Pisces

Biggest Smile—Leo

Most Attractive—Libra, Taurus

Best Liars—Gemini

Best Parents—Cancer

Pickiest In Love—Virgo, Capricorn

Most Generous—Leo

Best Manipulator—Scorpio

Most Charming—Libra, Sagittarius

Best Pick-Up Lines—Aries

Most Believable Pick-up Lines—Sagittarius

Most One-Nighters—Aries

Most Sensuous—Taurus

Most Pleasing—Pisces

Most Adult Film Stars—Scorpio, Leo

Most Friendly—Aquarius

Most Humanitarian—Aquarius, Gemini

Biggest Jewelry Boxes—Leo

Biggest Drinkers—Leo, Pisces

Best Criminal Mind—Scorpio, Gemini

Best Used-Car Salesman—Gemini

Most Millionaires—Cancer, Pisces

Most Workaholics—Leo, Capricorn

Bossiest—Leo, Cancer

Most Creative—Gemini, Libra, Leo

Most Psychic—Cancer, Pisces, Scorpio

Best Gossipers—Virgo, Gemini

Most Whiners—Pisces, Virgo

Best Homemaker/House Husband—
Cancer

Most Computer Savvy—Aquarius

Best Teachers—Gemini, Virgo

Best Doctors—Virgo, Scorpio

CHAPTER FIFTEEN

Maria's New Millennium Forecasts

Aries

Aries will find romance, love and creativity in abundance beginning with the summer of 2002. Cupid's arrow will continue to hit until August 2003. If single, this is a great time for the Ram to look for love. This is not a time to necessarily settle down but to play the field. In 2004–2005, the prospect of marriage is more appealing and timely.

Late July, August, late September and October are generally good times for Aries to find true love and make relationships a priority. If attached, the Aries can work on strengthening the bond in the first half of the decade. Expansion in the family is a possibility from 2001–2003 as well moving and relocation opportunities. Gambling and investments are a good bet in winter of 2003, and there are career peaks in 2008.

Taurus

The heavy energy Taurus was under from 1998 to early 2001 has lifted. The bulls should enjoy money making opportunities but are cautioned to invest wisely. Real estate may be a good investment. Their love lives fare well in late summer and late fall each year, but real romance hits around the middle of the decade and culminates in 2006.

Home and family issues prove to be positive, although the career path seems uncertain and changeable. Taurus will be learning many new things about themselves and their world.

New hobbies and pleasure activities will become a popular pastime in 2004 when Bulls get out of their lazy-boy chairs and experiment with creative pursuits and sports. In 2005, they get more recognition among co-workers and feel empowered on the job. 2007 could also be a strong financial year. There may be windfalls from legal settlements, inheritances and joint accounts.

Gemini

The fun starts early on and continues for the first two years of the new millennium. Then it's time to roll up the sleeves and get down to work until mid-2003. The foundations Gemini lay during these 2.5 years will likely influence the rest of the decade for them. Make your choices wisely, Gemini. You've noticed your likes and dislikes have been changing when it comes to relationships. What you wanted or needed from love in the past is not necessary anymore. It's out with the old and in with new. Love comes around the holidays, Thanksgiving through Christmas.

Best years to find a soul mate are 2003–2004 and 2007. The financial picture looks bright in 2002, but it's a good idea to put some away, for you'll need a rainy-day account more than once in the following two years. A new career path may be on the horizon by the middle of the decade, and you'll emerge feeling more creative and energized than ever before!

Cancer

You'll be feeling especially secure and happy, Cancer, from mid-2001 to 2002. Relationship smoke signals fire up around Halloween and New Year's each year. But the luckiest times in love are 2006 and 2008

During the first few years of the new millennium there's a maturing of your soul, Cancer, so let bygones be bygones. You're stirring up and releasing old hurts and pains on the subconscious levels. This will help raise you to new heights and awareness. You can make the most of career, family and love.

There may be transformations in the workplace, especially among co-workers. Health issues that may appear, no matter how small, should be taken care of.

Money grows on trees in 2002–2003, but be careful, Cancer, of overspending, by 2005. You'll wish you saved some of it. Remodeling or moving and expansion of the family circle takes center stage in 2005. You may even decide you want two places to call home. A home on the lake would suit you just fine!

Leo

Unexpected changes in your personal relationship may leave you feeling a little apprehensive about love the next few years. Don't worry Leo. Your heart is strong and you're a survivor. By the time this decade's over, you could have found true, everlasting, divine love. Career is on a fast track in the first few years and the friends you meet in 2001 to 2003 could last a lifetime. The spotlight will be on you from 2002 to 2003. Make the most of it, turn it up and let it shine. You'll be meeting some very creative, unusual people over the next few years. Romance is nice through the Christmas season and around February every year.

Financial rewards are strong in 2004, a carry-over from your most luckiest years, but gambling habits should be kept to a minimum until 2007, when lady luck again shines upon you.

Virgo

2001 to mid-2003 could leave you indecisive about your career direction, Virgo. There are wonderful blessings coming your way in regard to your life's work. Unfortunately, you could become a victim in a relationship over the course of the next few years, so be aware of whom you make promises to. January and March are often times to seek love, but the first half of the decade is better to seek approval and recognition from the outside world, rather than from intimate circles.

You've been working very hard and this is the time for payoffs. Changes with your home may take place until 2005. You're learning to stand up for yourself like never before in relationships. Being the giver that you are, you're now learning that it's important for you to receive. Allow yourself to do so.

There could be more than one love interest around you. Choose wisely.

Libra

Expect the unexpected in the area of love affairs. You'll be meeting people in the most unlikely places and when you least expect to so make sure you look your best at all times! Also, do not judge a book by its cover. You could be played a fool by lovers if you're not careful. Growth comes in the form of career opportunities and promotions from 2001 to

2005 and new friends enter the picture in 2003. Expect romantic advances in February and April. Higher education and travel to exotic foreign spots look inviting until 2003. Luck with money hits in 2006, but 2005 is a many-blessing year, too!

In 2006, your creative urges soar, and you could make money from an artistic idea. You'll feel more like traveling, joining groups and making new friends than ever before in 2003, and those new acquaintances could be very supportive of your career and life path.

Scorpio

Scorpios have already had all of their buttons pushed over the last several decades. Now it's time for a breather and good fortune. Career goals can be achieved in 2003 to 2007 in bigger ways than ever imagined if you're ready.

Relationships should be working out by now, considering the chaos in the late 90s and early 2000.

Changes are forthcoming in the career field. They are inevitable, yet very profitable for you, Scorpio, and could help you get the fame and fortune you deserve. The way you feel about financial security and money needs are changing, too.

Expect 2006 to be a very good year all around. Relationships for the most part look stable, but there may be unexpected changes within the home life. Relocation, remodeling, new purchases and additions to the family are all part of the Scorpio scenarios for coming years.

Sagittarius

The new millennium kicks off with good luck in the area of romance, especially marriage. Make sure any or all gnawing issues are resolved by 2002 or there could be trouble in paradise.

Partnerships of all types are favored during the early part of 2001. If legal matters arise, they should be favorable. More doors are open to you that were once closed. Don't be too proud to ask for help. People will be more than happy to oblige.

Many deep psychological changes are happening in your psyche, Sagittarius. You will feel as if a part of you has died and there is a rebirth. A new and improved "you" is emerging.

The spring and early summer months of 2001 are nice for love. 2004 could prove to be a tremendous year for career gain and notoriety. Your pocketbook swells in 2002 and 2008.

Capricorn

Committed relationships, marriage and strong, devoted partnerships are highlighted from 2001 to 2002. Be warned of partnerships problems, however from 2003 to 2005. May and

July are always good for seeking out that special someone. Don't be too cautious. Allow yourself to take risks in the fall of 2001. You'll have the energy and drive to accomplish great things!

Money comes from unusual sources or with the advent of new ideas. Be open to change, and you'll see your earnings soar! Going back to school, attending conferences and workshops in 2004 will help put you in line for a career promotion the following year. Don't discount lessons you learned from your past to help you with the future.

Aquarius

A more spiritually enlightened Aquarius is emerging over the next few years. Be open to what the universe has to tell you and wishes to bring you. Love affairs take off early in the decade, but true commitments are solid in 2003. Job changes are likely in 2002 to 2005, especially in the areas of service work. Late spring through late summer, are good times to look for love. Watch out for weight gain in 2002, but you could work on improving health issues at the same time. Legal issues or obligations could arise in mid-2000. The earlier you meet them, the better. You may suffer from identity problems at time but the entire decade is good for spiritual awakening and getting in tune with your higher self. After all, this is the Age of Aquarius.

Pisces

Pisces people will find expansion within the home and family the first part of the decade. By 2006, they will be at a peak in their career, if they've worked hard and laid good foundations during the six years prior.

Many are feeling they want to transform their lives. It's as if the universe is gently nudging them into a new direction. Many Pisces will change career paths over the course of the next few years. Love knocks at their door in summer of 2001 to 2003. Commitments are favored in 2004. July and September are nice romantic times. The troubling money times in the late 90s should be thing of the past if they spend wisely.

2002–2003 is a fine time to reevaluate goals and life direction. Love affairs will also play a big role in Pisces' lives at this time. Children and creative hobbies or talents are emphasized during the same years.